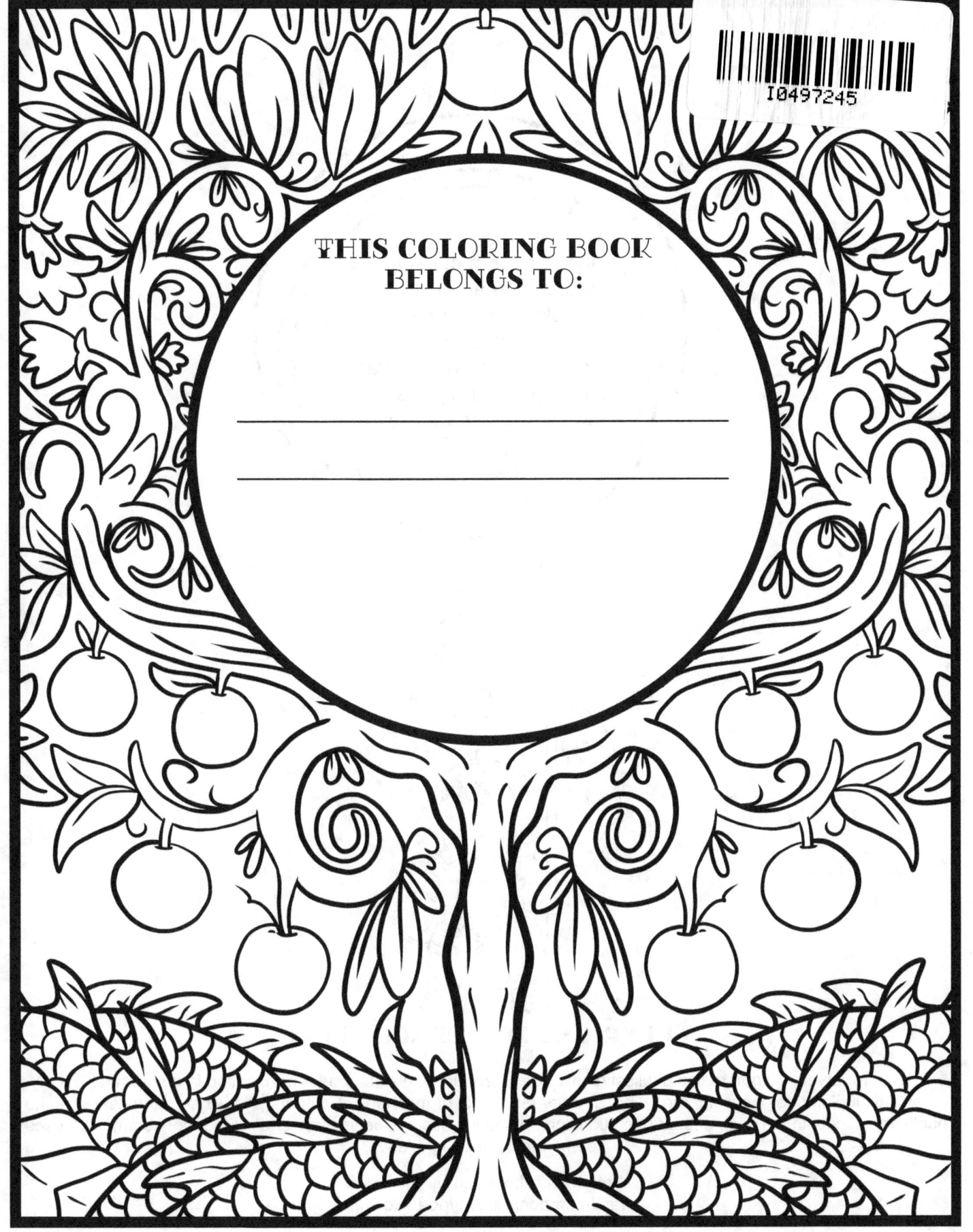

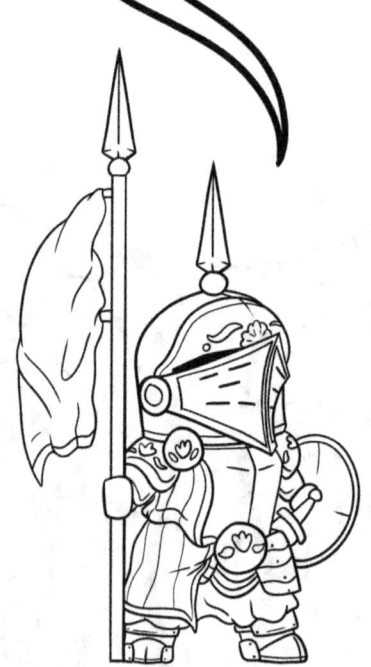

Hello, my name is Sir Sprout and I am on a quest for fruit dragons. You and I will observe and color them together. If you need the name, or an fun fact, look to the **back** of the dragons' page. If you cut a page out, the fun information will stay with that dragon. For extra details feel free to explore and research!

COPYRIGHT 2021 DRACO FRUIT

All rights reserved, no part of this publication may be reproduced, distributed, or transmitted in any form or by any means, including photocopying, recording, or other electronic or mechanical, without prior written permission of the publisher, except in the case of brief quotations embodied in critical reviews and certain other noncommercial uses permitted by copyright law.

Written and illustrated by Jill Jones
wacomdragonartist.myportfolio.com

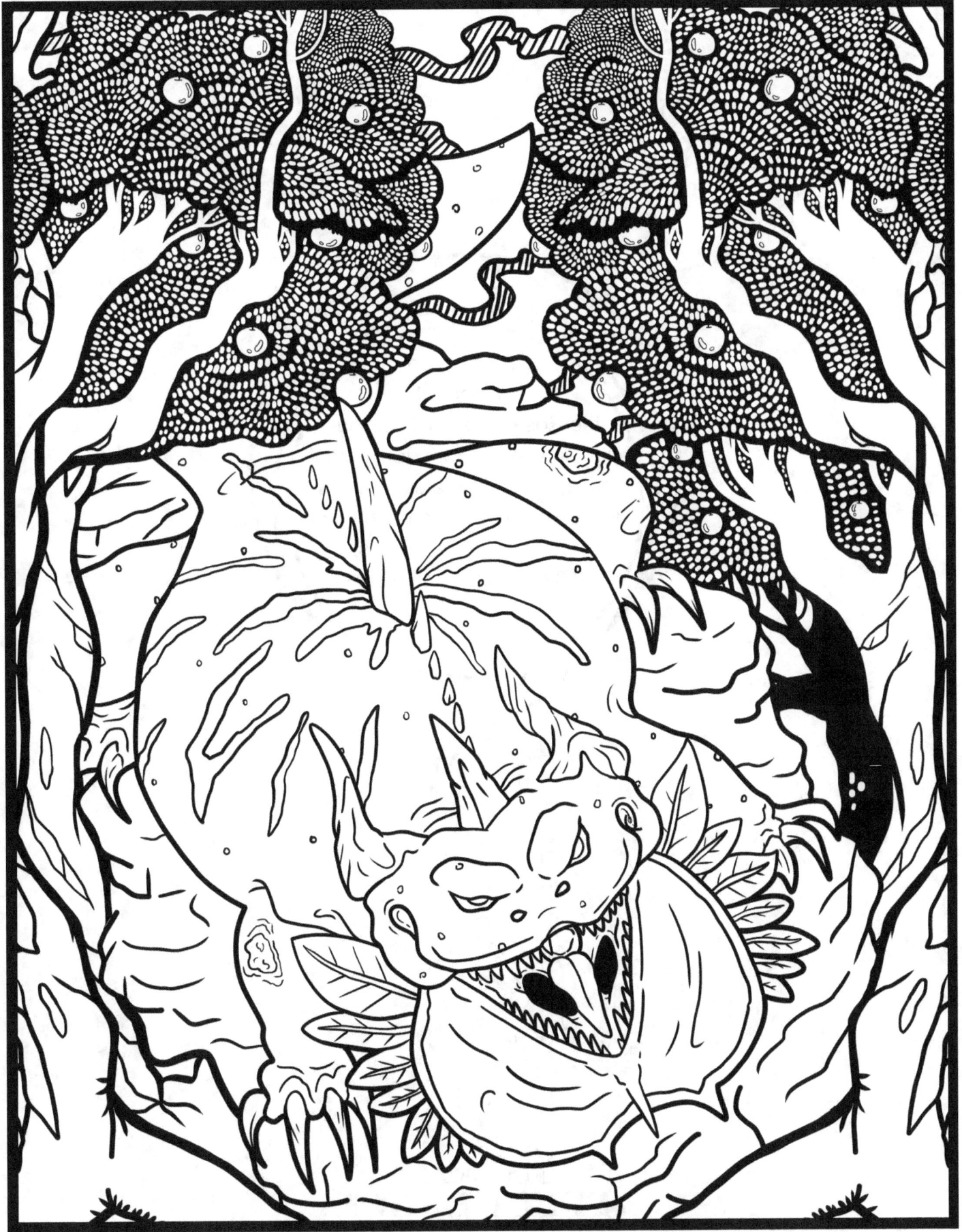

Apples are a member of the Rosaceae family, along with many other important crops. Yes, apples are related to roses; give your loved one a bouquet of apples instead of roses. Beautiful and edible!

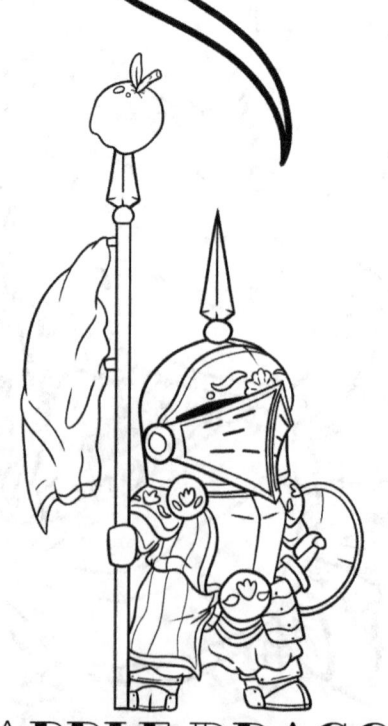

APPLE DRAGON

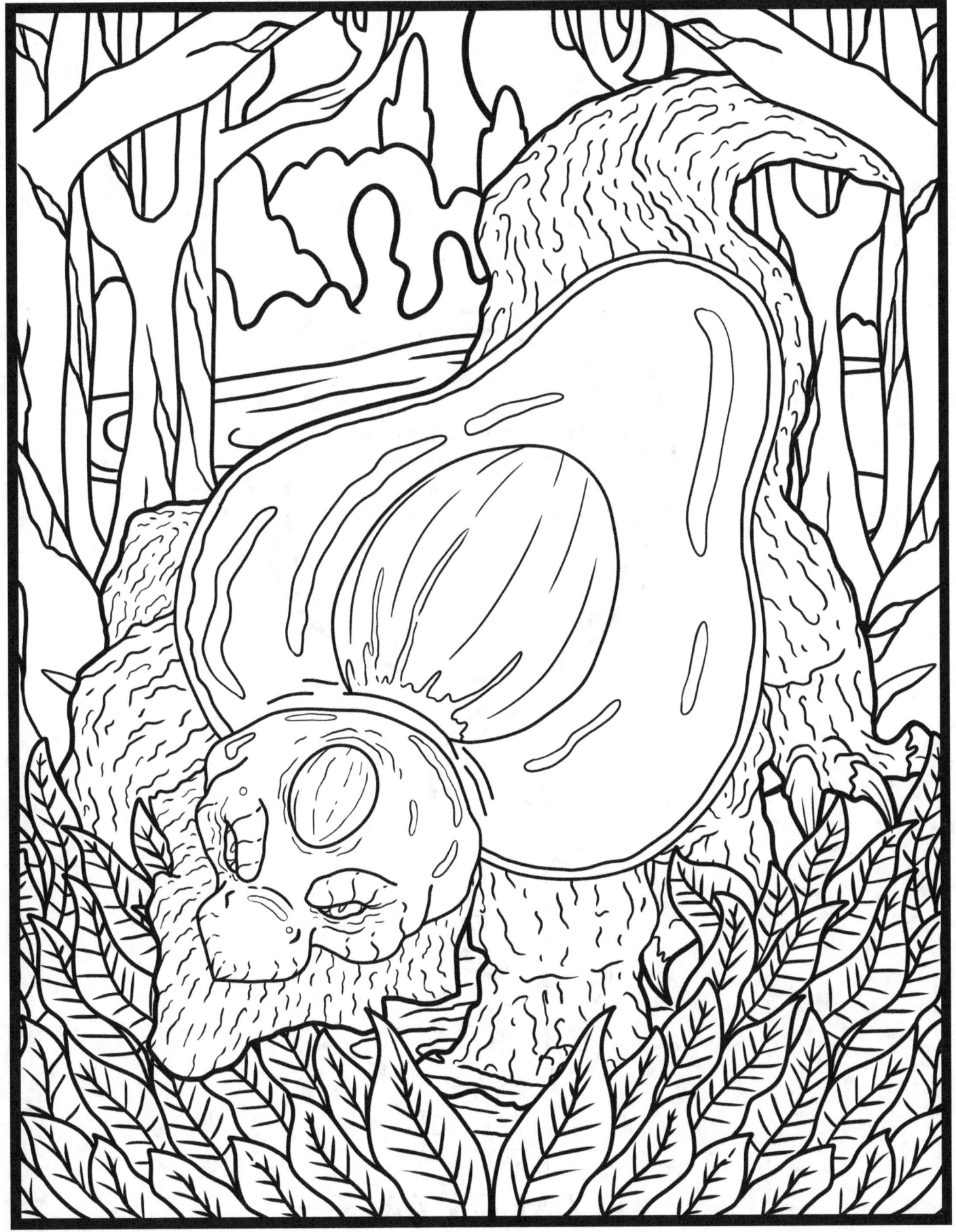

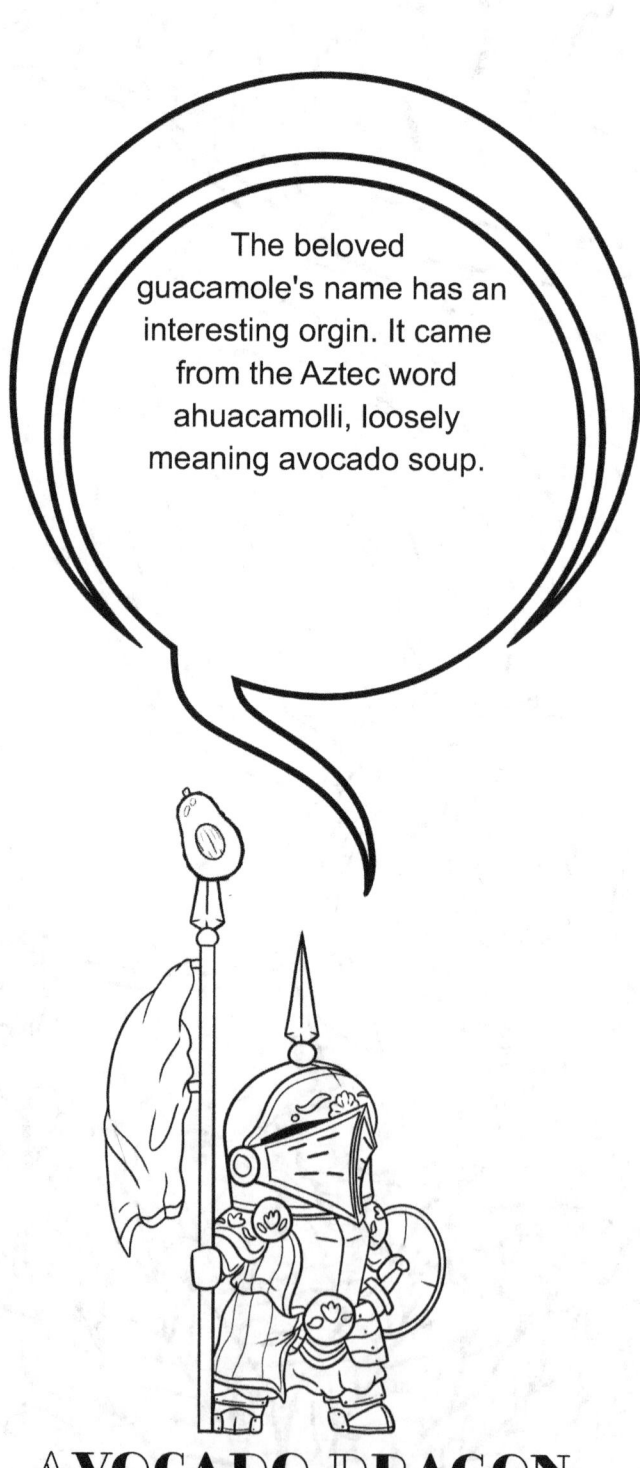

AVOCADO DRAGON

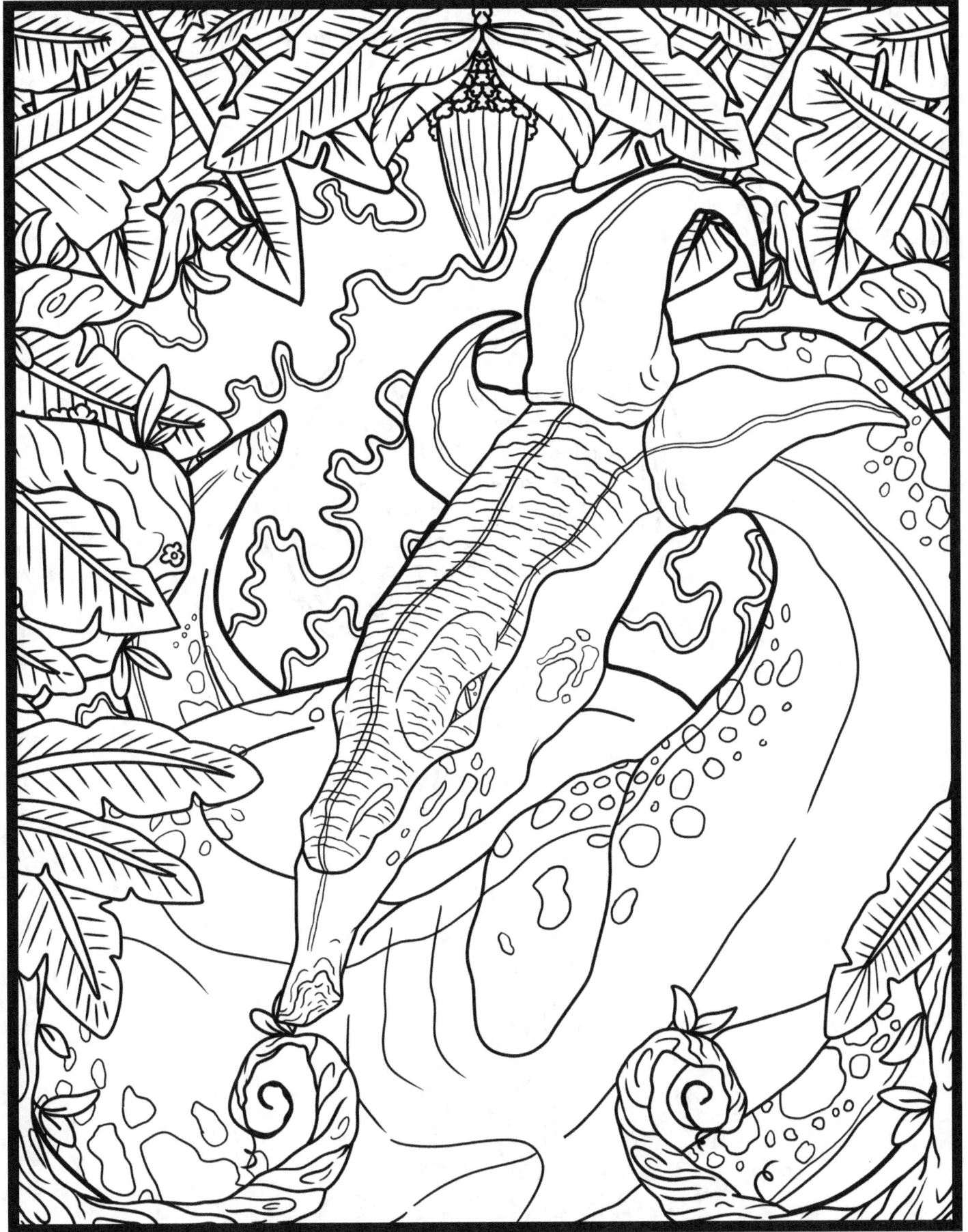

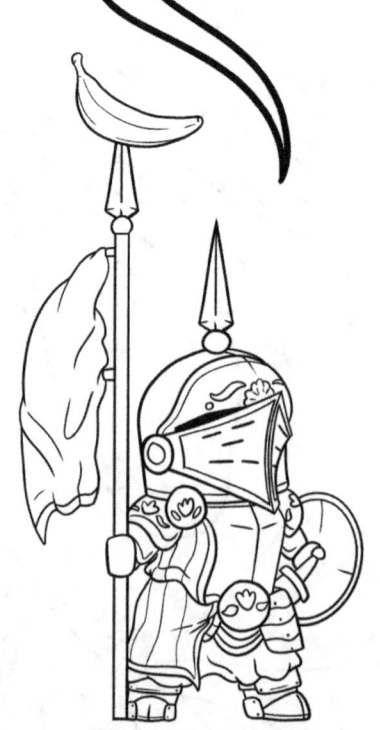

BANANA DRAGON

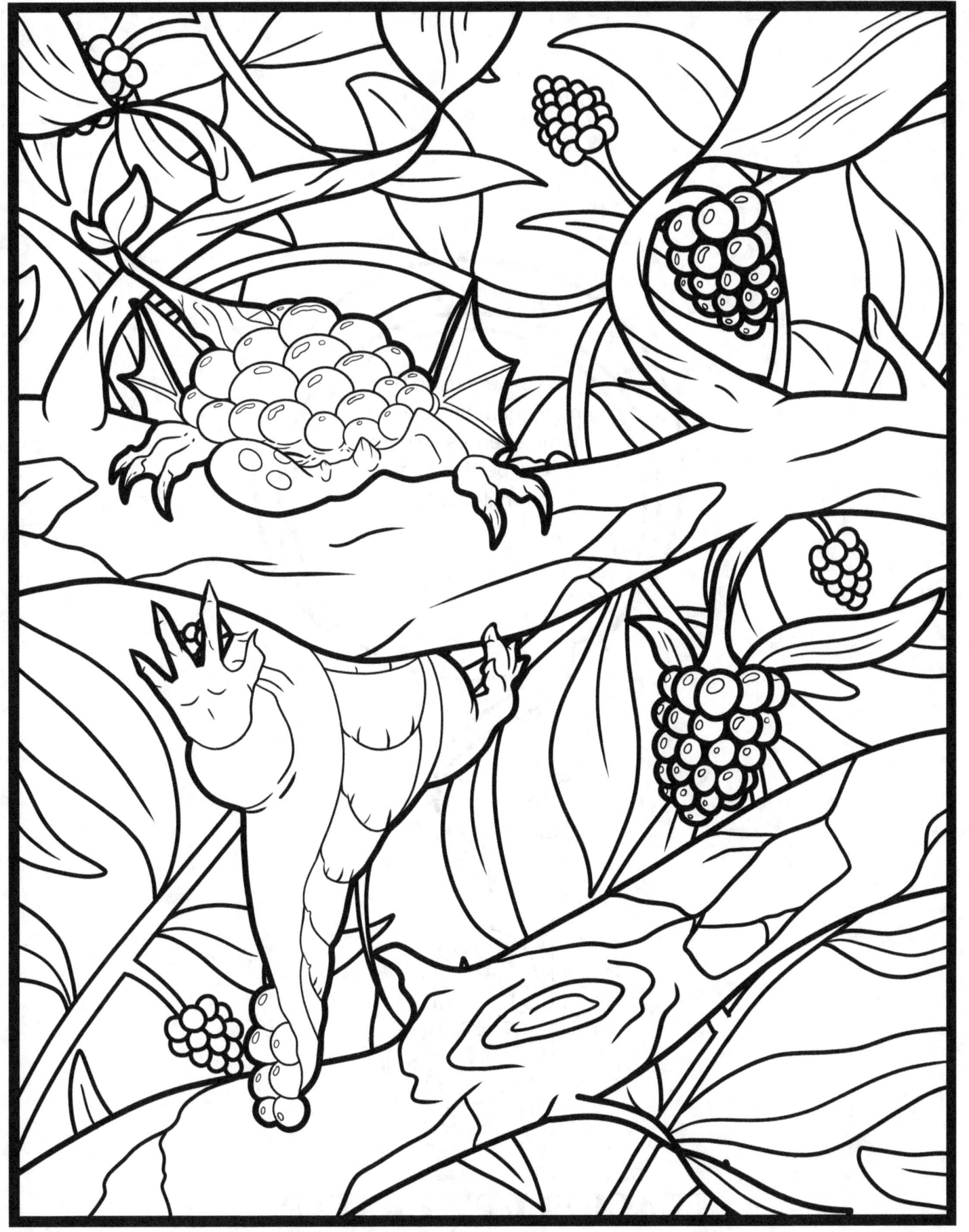

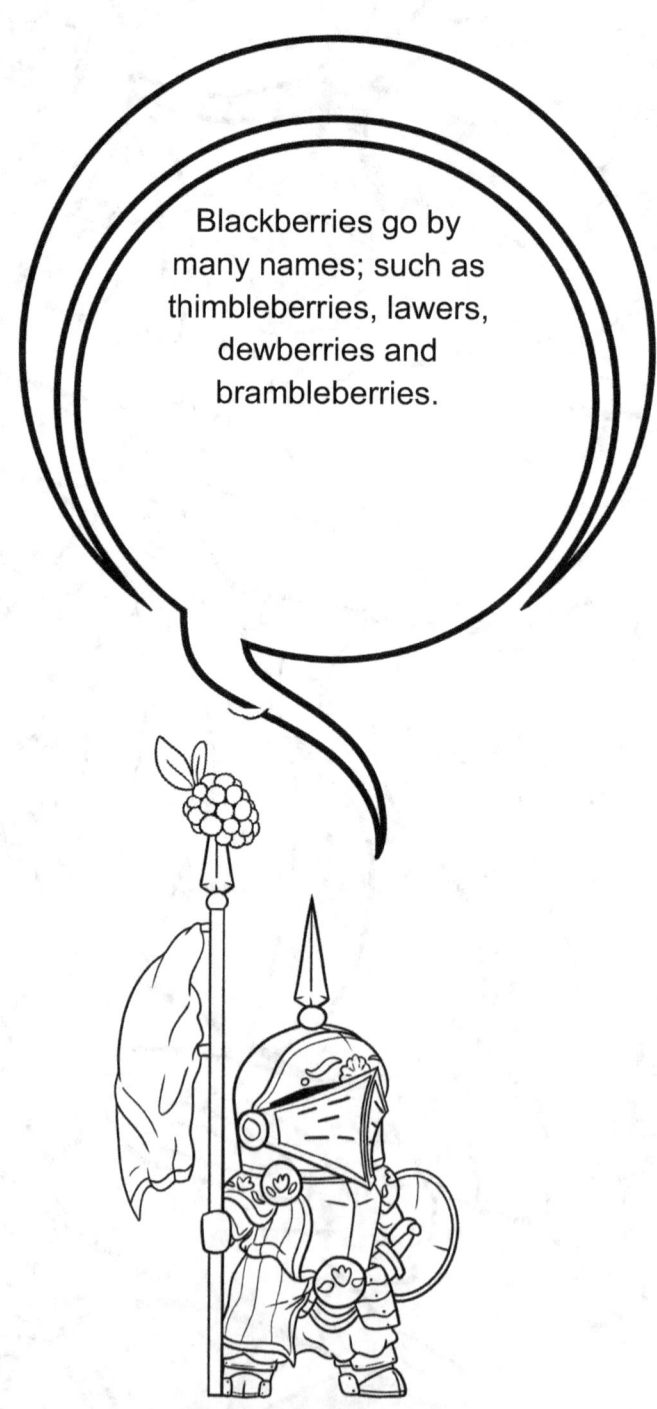

BLACKBERRY DRAGON

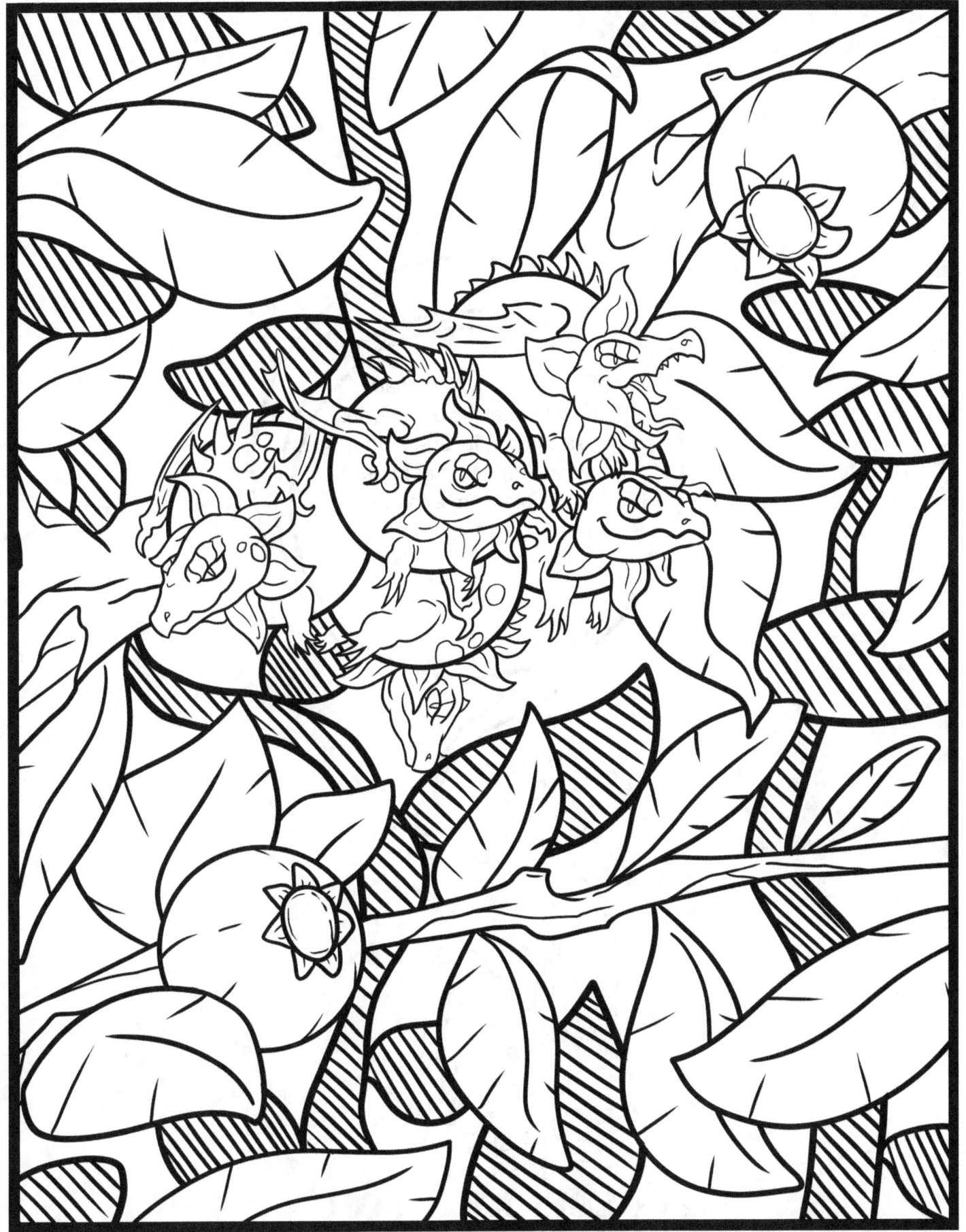

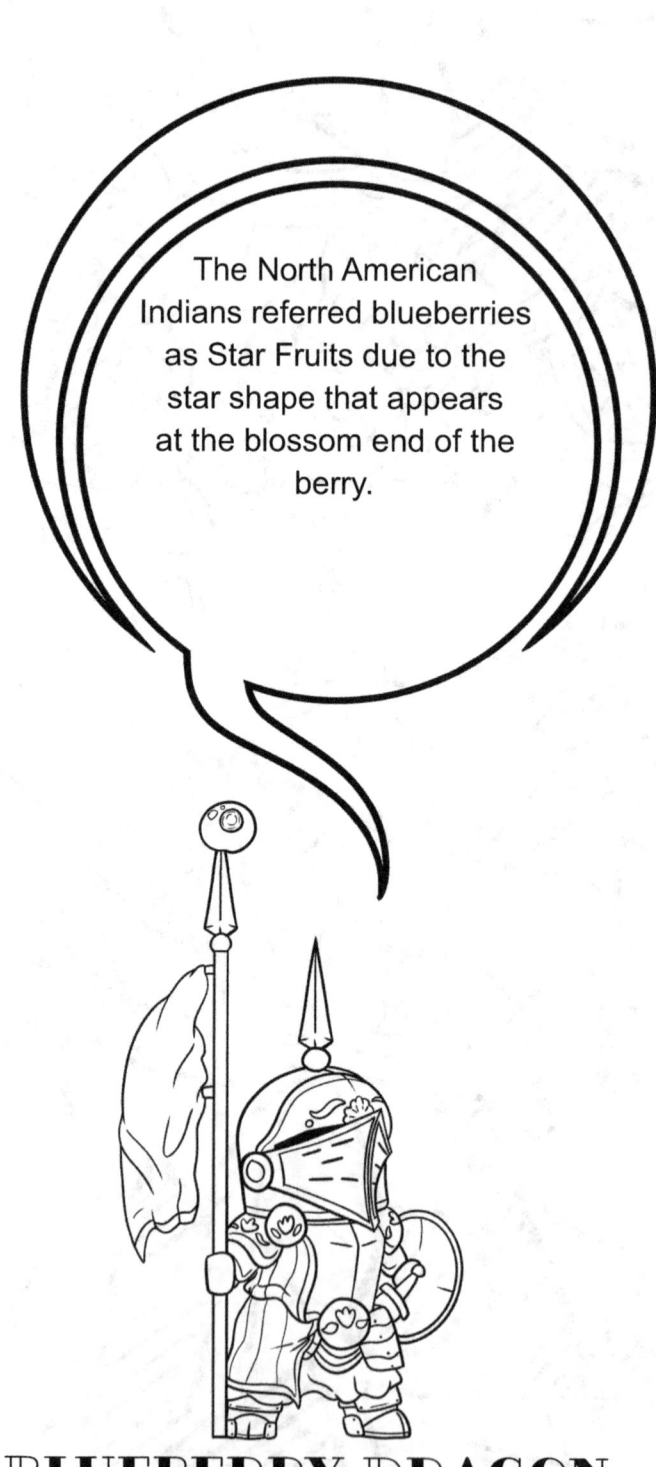

The North American Indians referred blueberries as Star Fruits due to the star shape that appears at the blossom end of the berry.

BLUEBERRY DRAGON

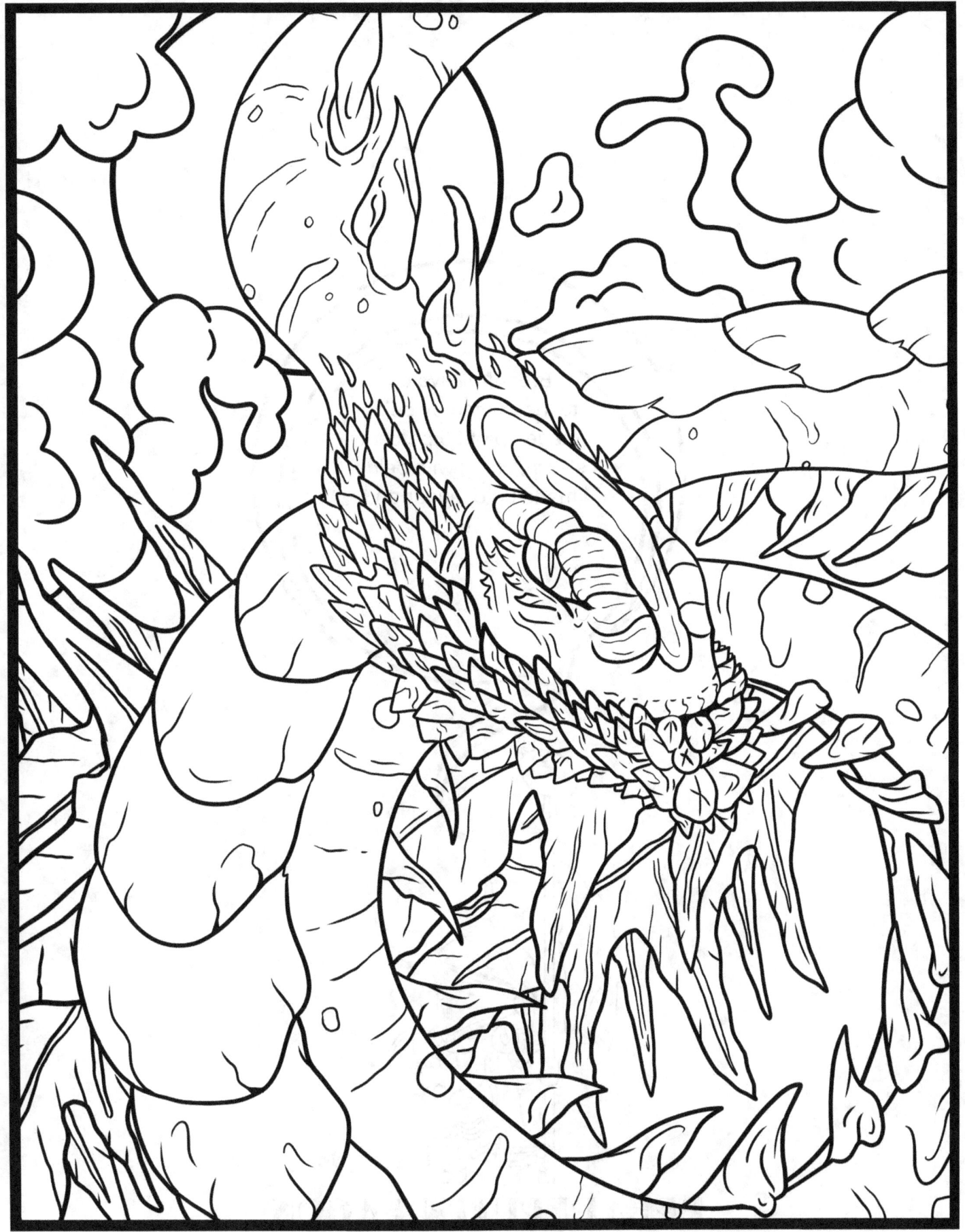

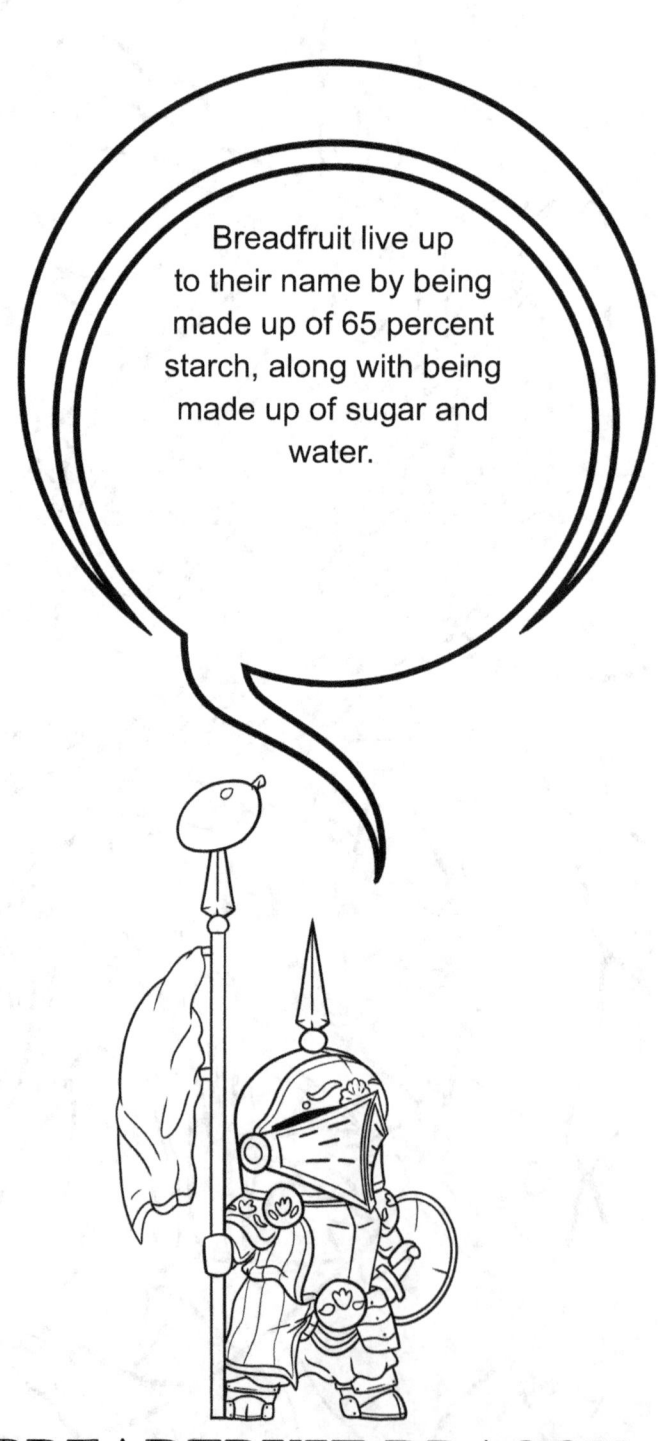

BREADFRUIT DRAGON

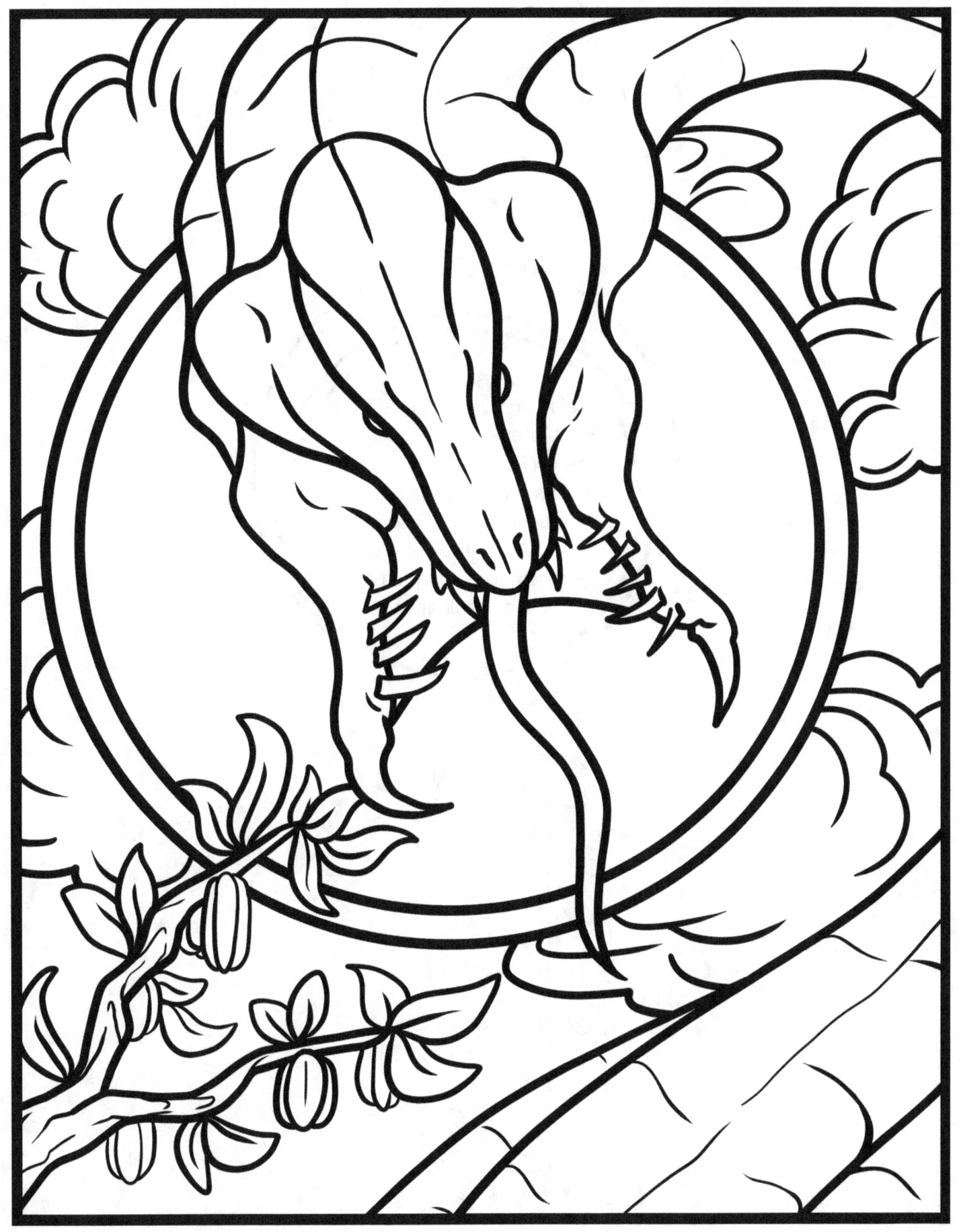

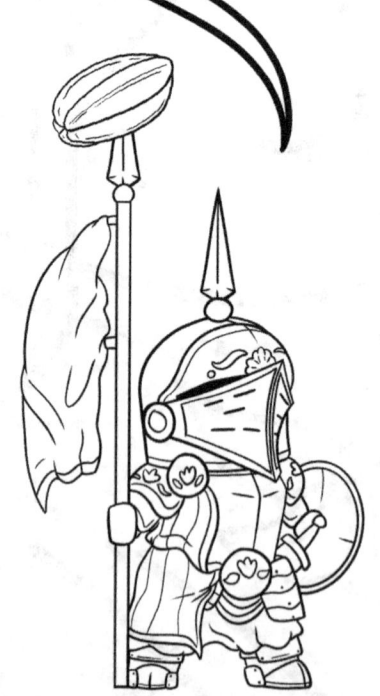

Carambola, also known as the Star Fruit, prevent the activity of the CYP3A4 enzyme. This enzyme is responsible for the absorption of 50% of all medications into the blood, so best to eat when not taking medications.

CARAMBOLA DRAGON

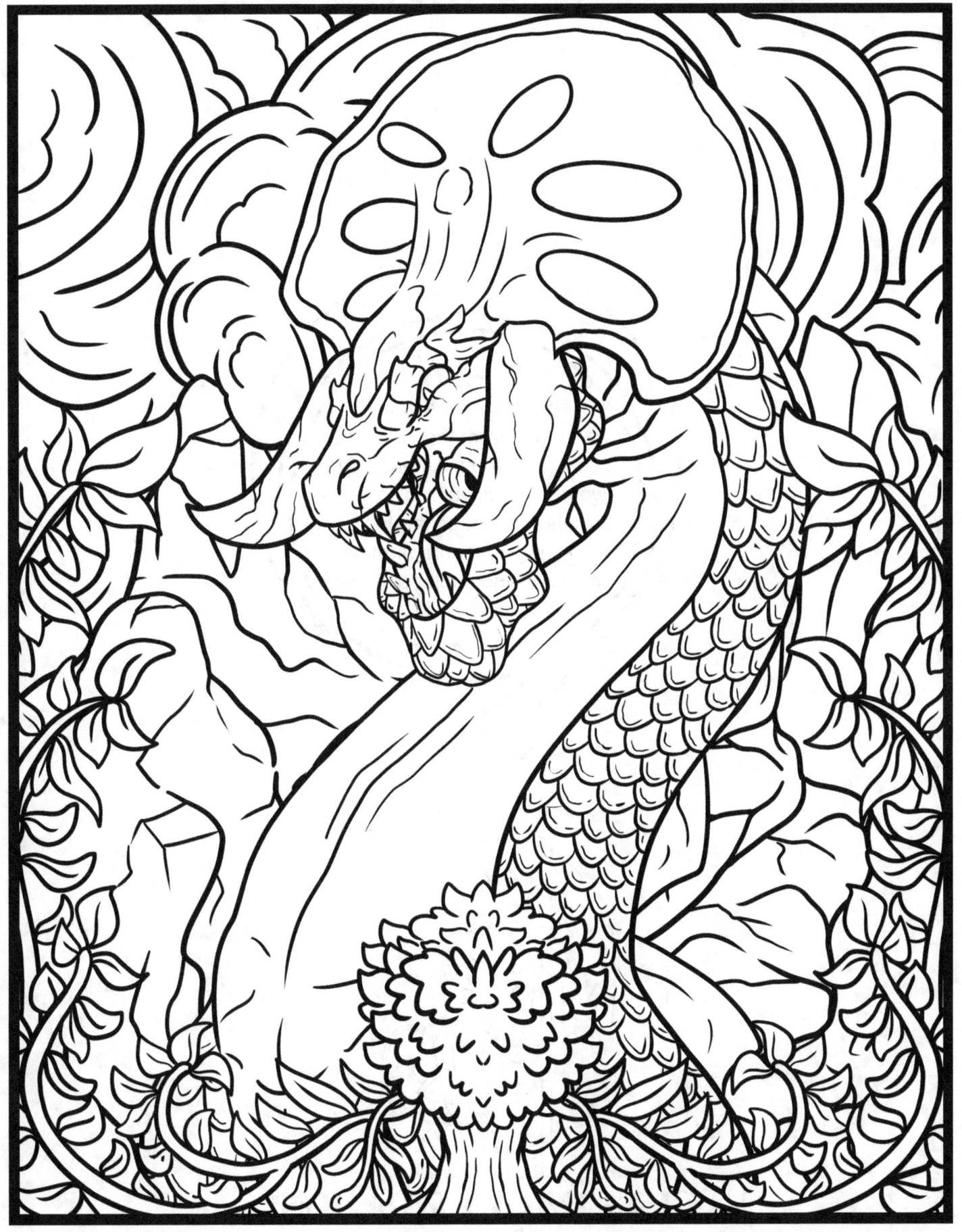

> The name derives from the Quechua language from the Quechua people, of South America. The word Cherimoya translates to cold seeds, due to the fact that the plant grows and germinates at higher and cooler altitudes.

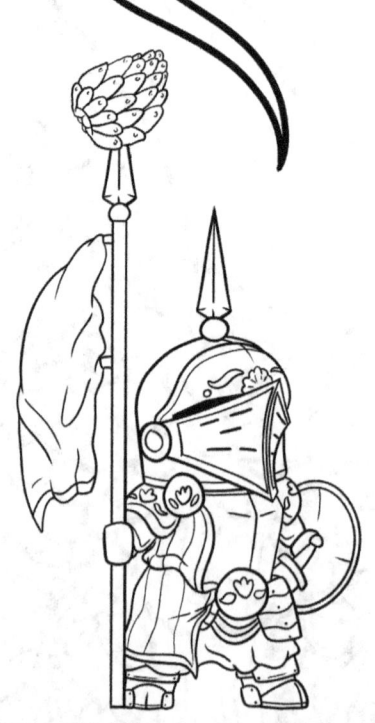

CHERIMOYA DRAGON

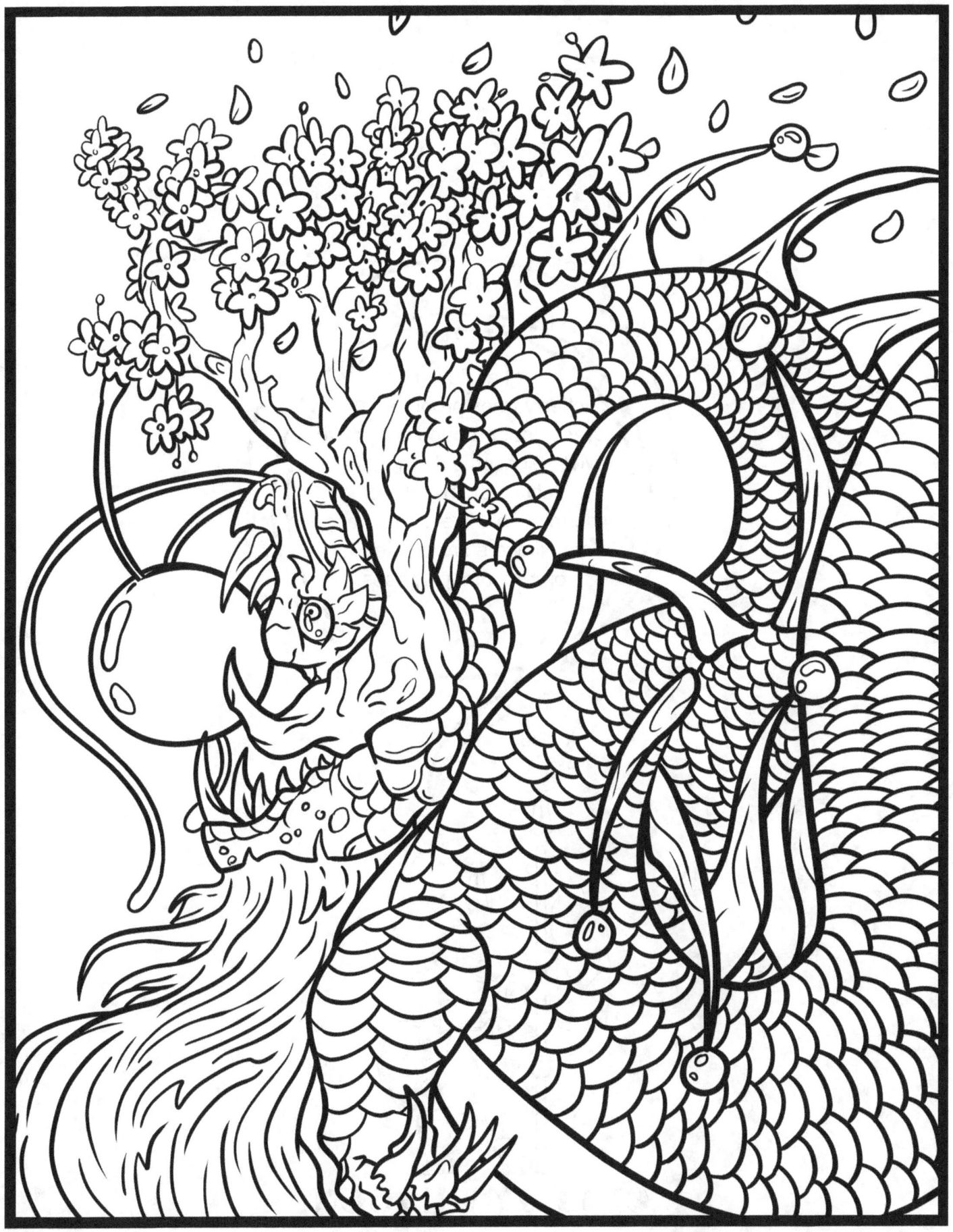

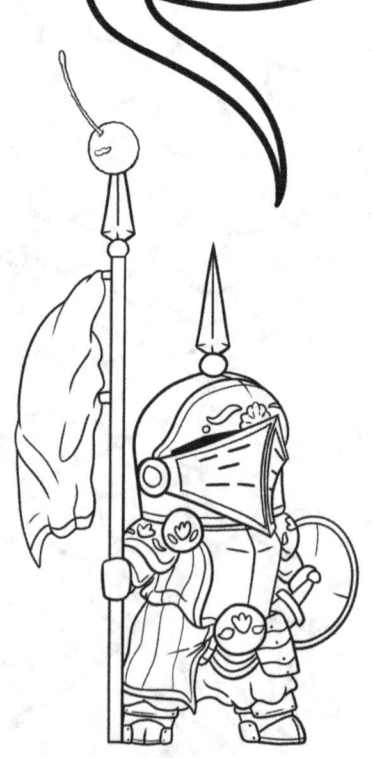

Not all flowering cherry trees produce fruit. Trees, that produce fruit, have white blossoms during spring relying on insects for germination. Trees that have pink flowers are planted for ornamental purposes.

CHERRY DRAGON

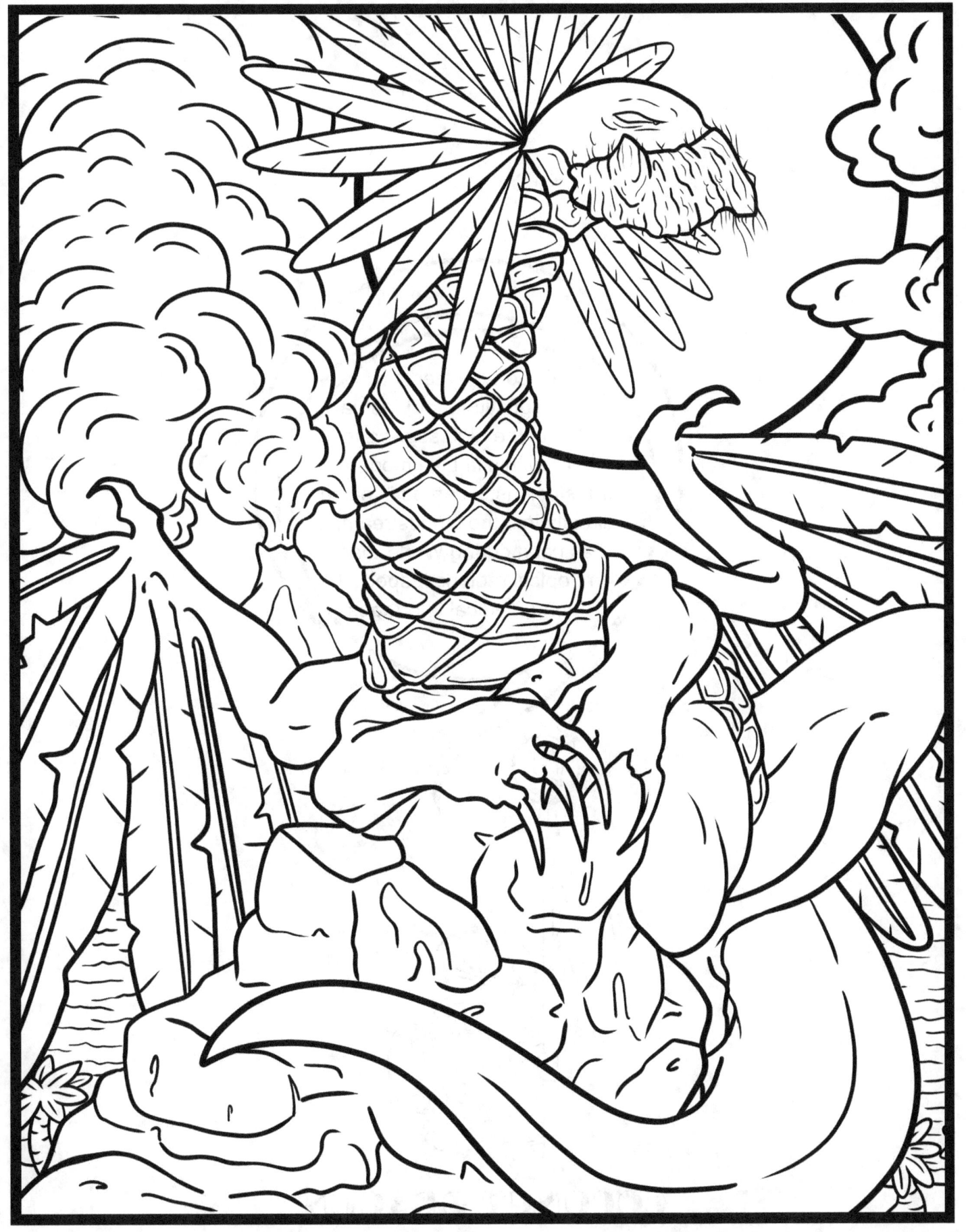

> Coconut water is a great substitute for plasma, due to the high sugar and salts within it. Like modern transfusions, it can be injected directly into the bloodstream. It was used during World War II in tropical regions, especially during medical shortages.

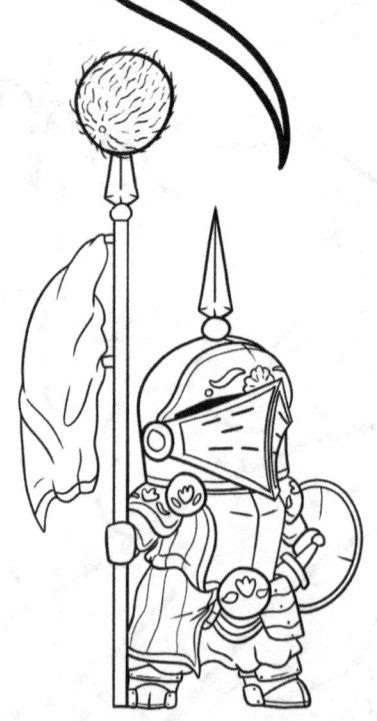

COCONUT DRAGON

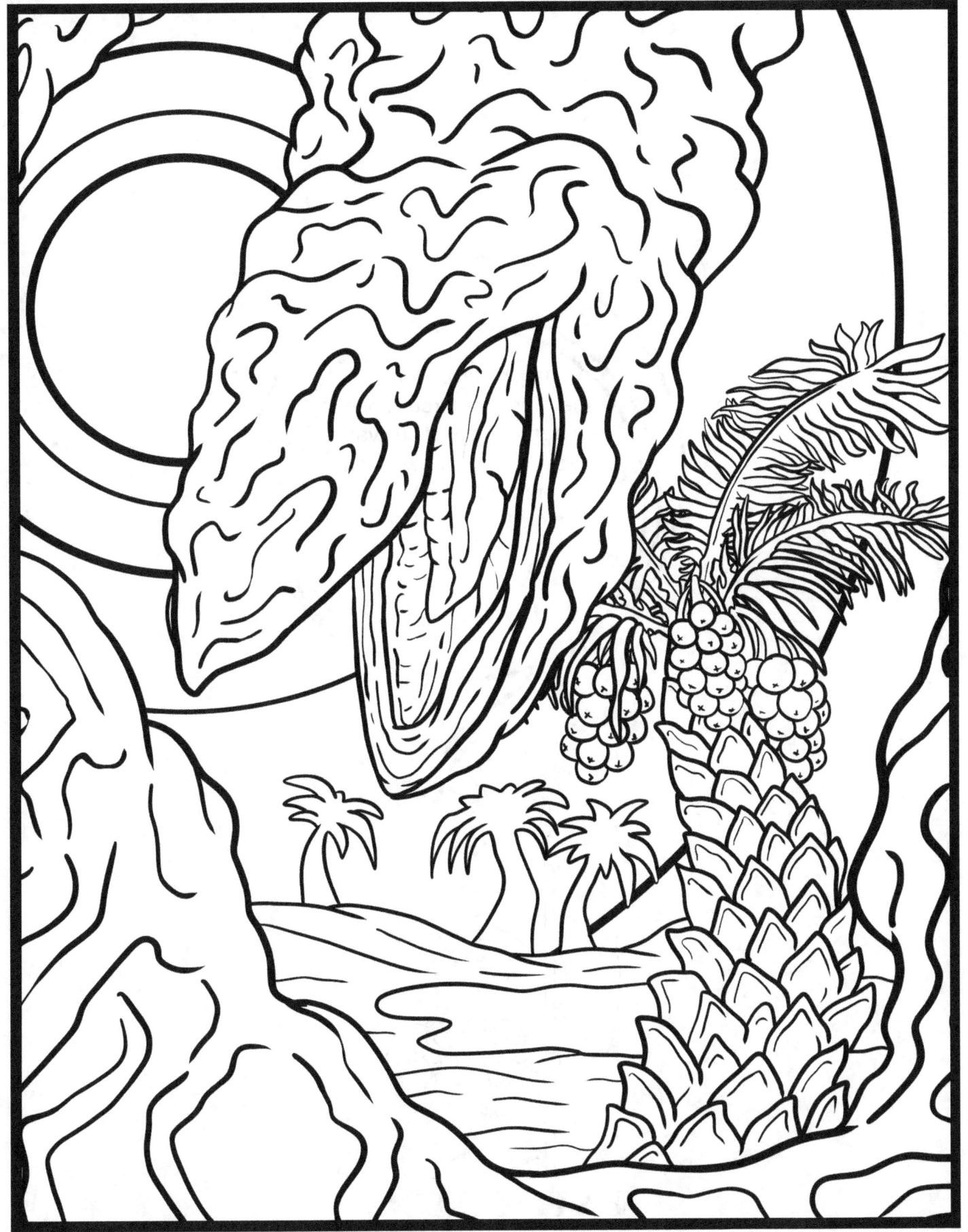

It is believed that the Date Palm tree is one of the most ancient cultivated trees, it's fruits have been harvested in North Africa and the Middle East for 5000 years.

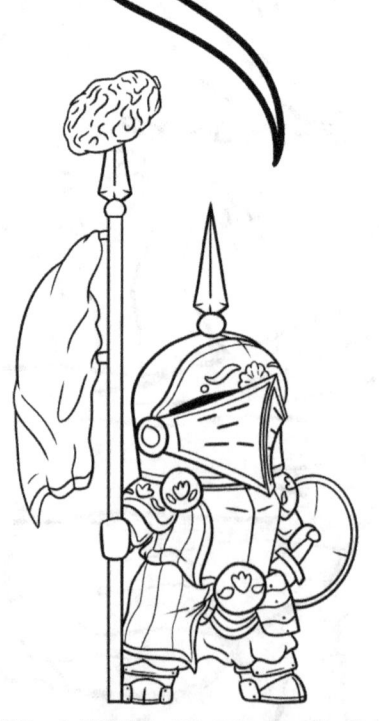

DATE DRAGON

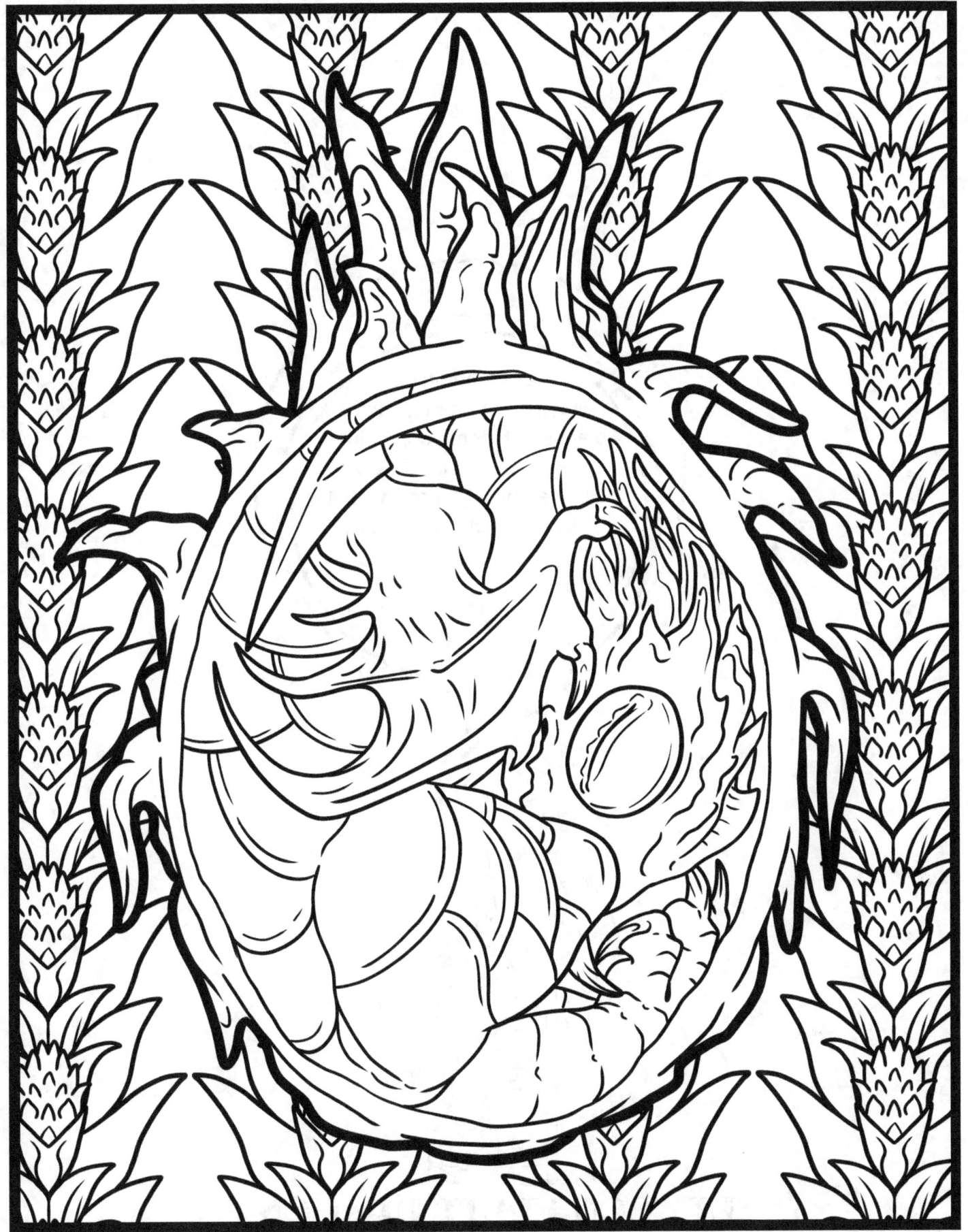

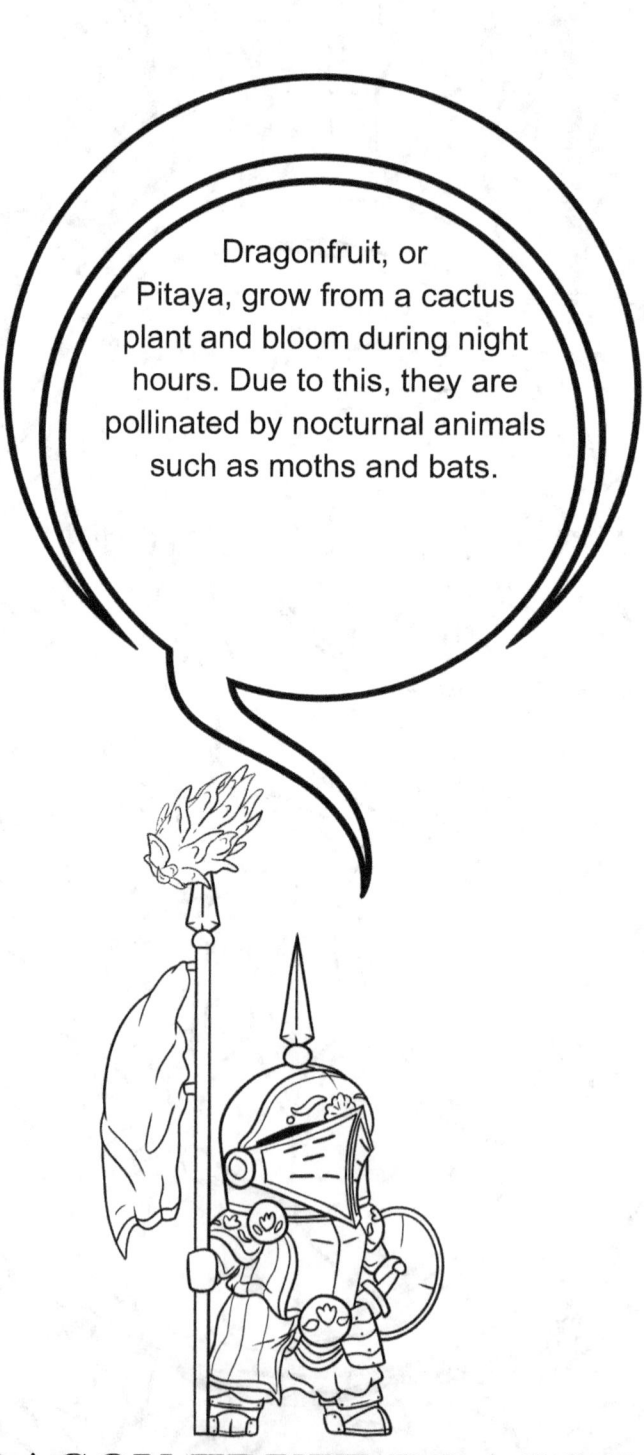

Dragonfruit, or Pitaya, grow from a cactus plant and bloom during night hours. Due to this, they are pollinated by nocturnal animals such as moths and bats.

DRAGON FRUIT DRAGON

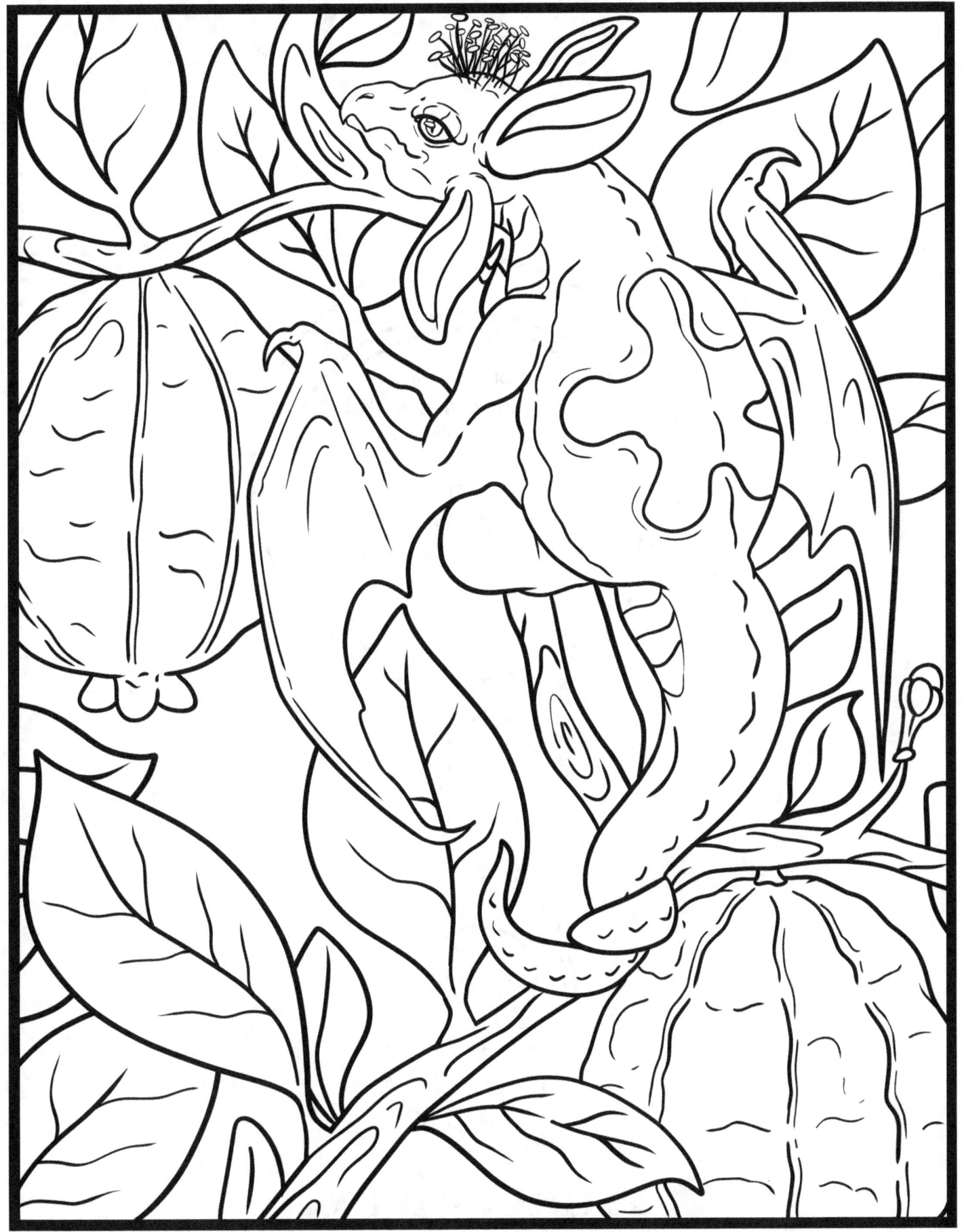

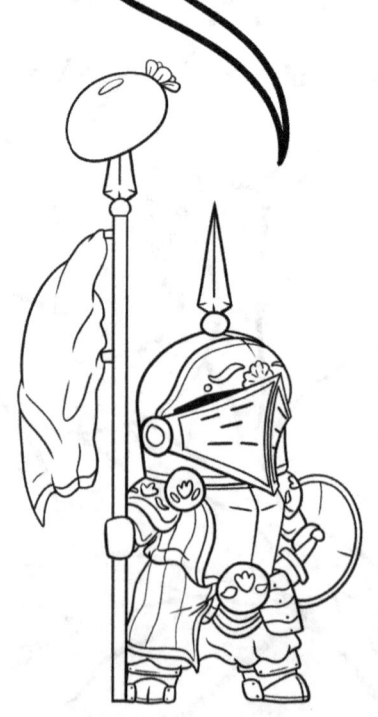

All of this fruit is edible, the center is filled with a sweet jelly which is surrounded by a soft gritty, pear-like flesh. The skin is also edible, though it can be a little too bitter for some people's pallet.

FEIJOA DRAGON

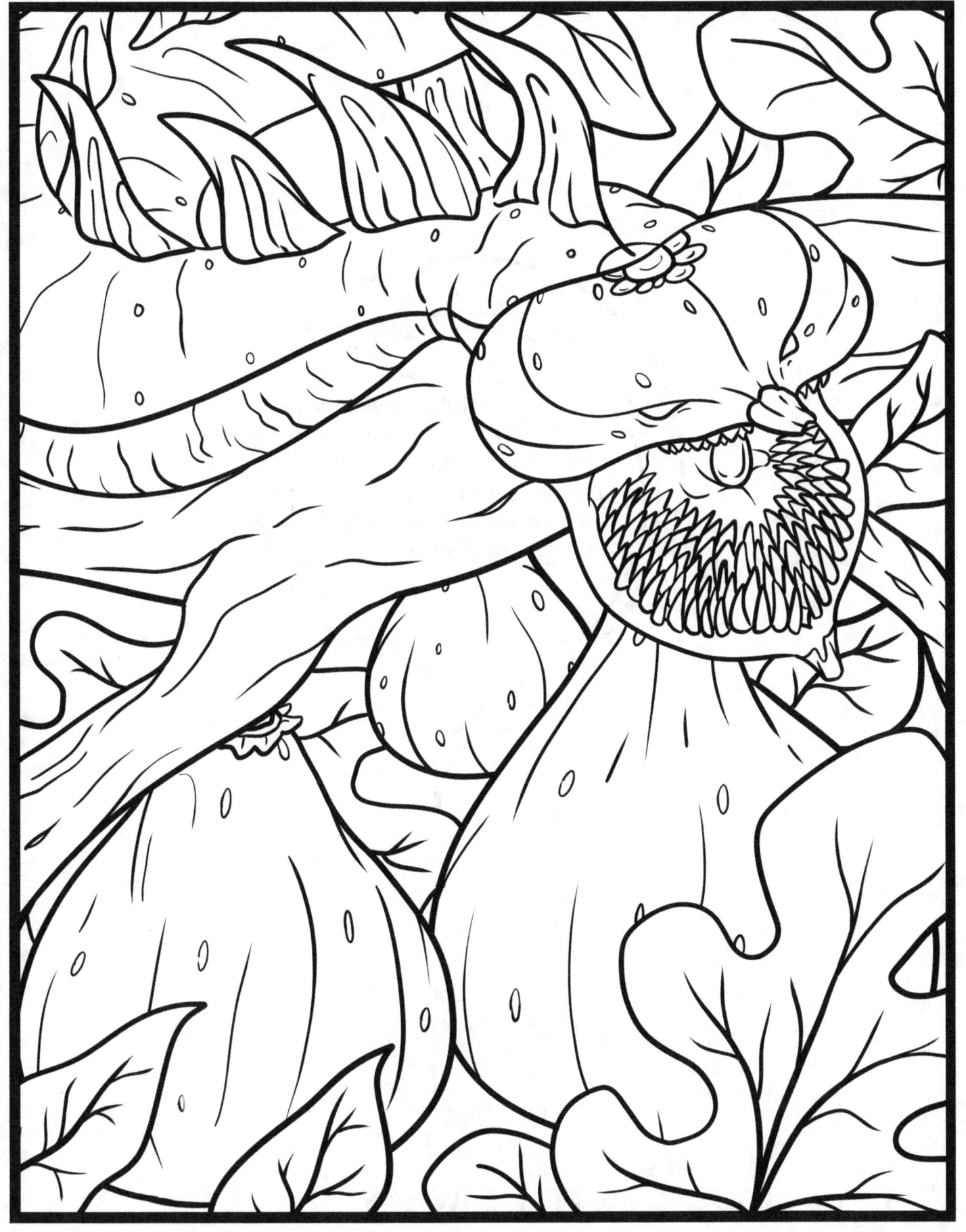

When a fig tree bloom, no visible flowers are seen. That is because the blossoms are within the fruit, producing the small crunchy seeds, resulting in the unique texture of the fruit.

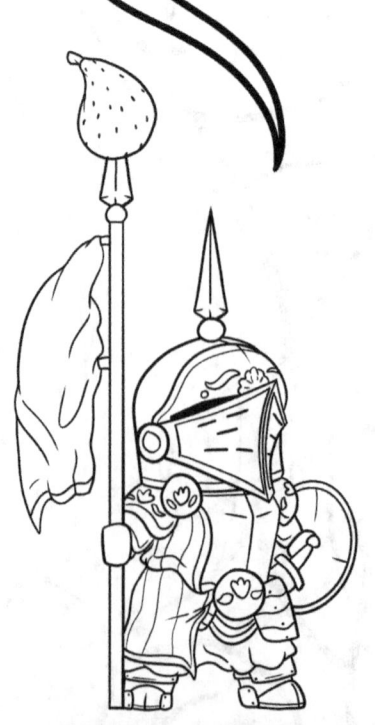

FIG DRAGON

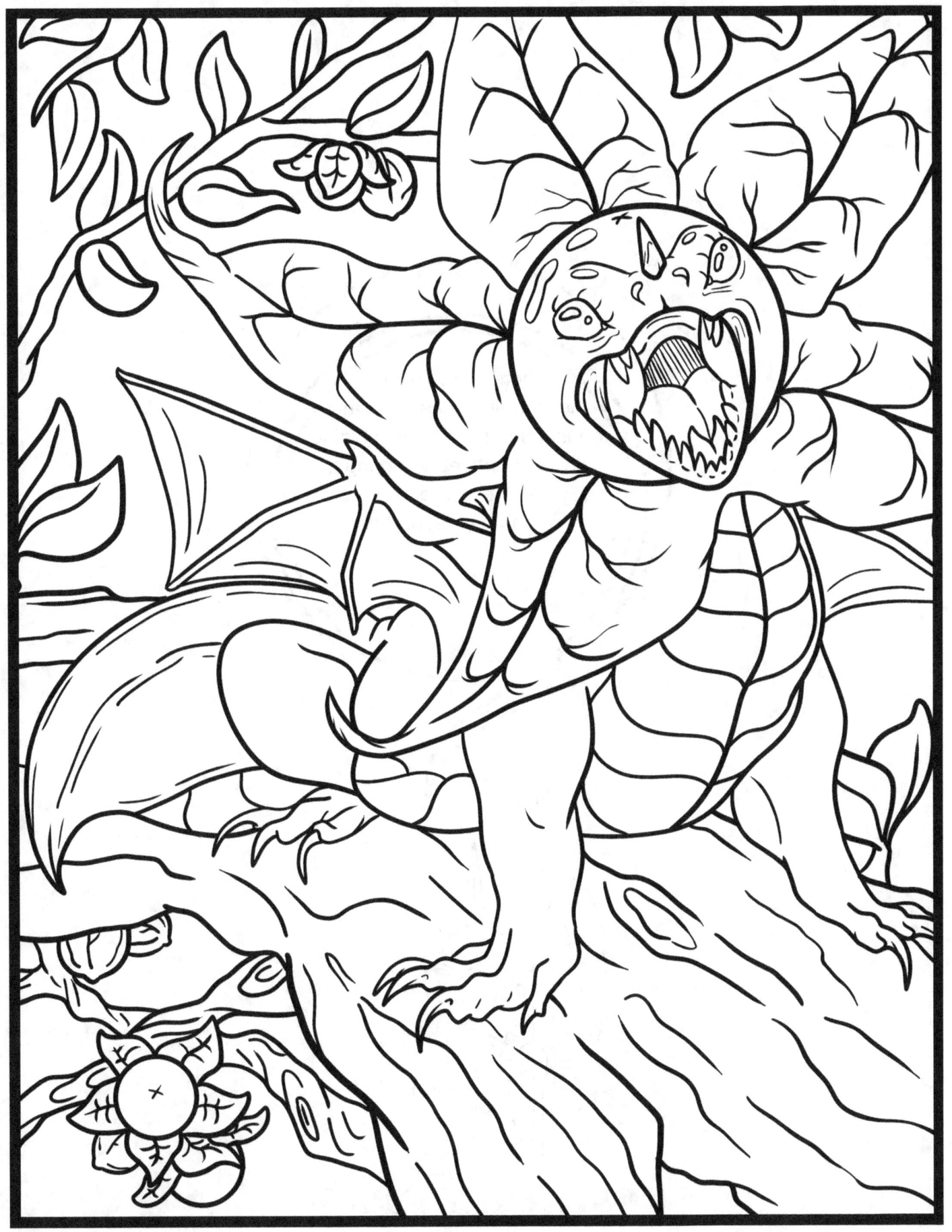

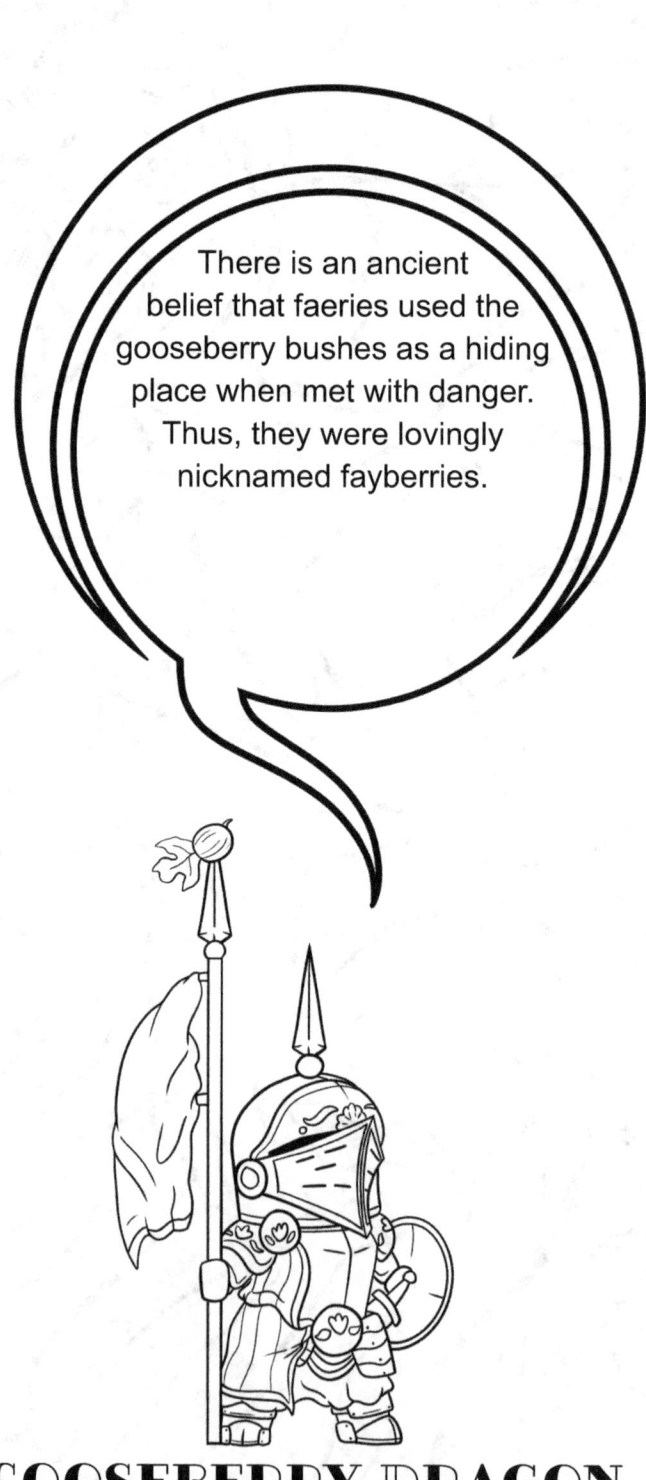

There is an ancient belief that faeries used the gooseberry bushes as a hiding place when met with danger. Thus, they were lovingly nicknamed fayberries.

GOOSEBERRY DRAGON

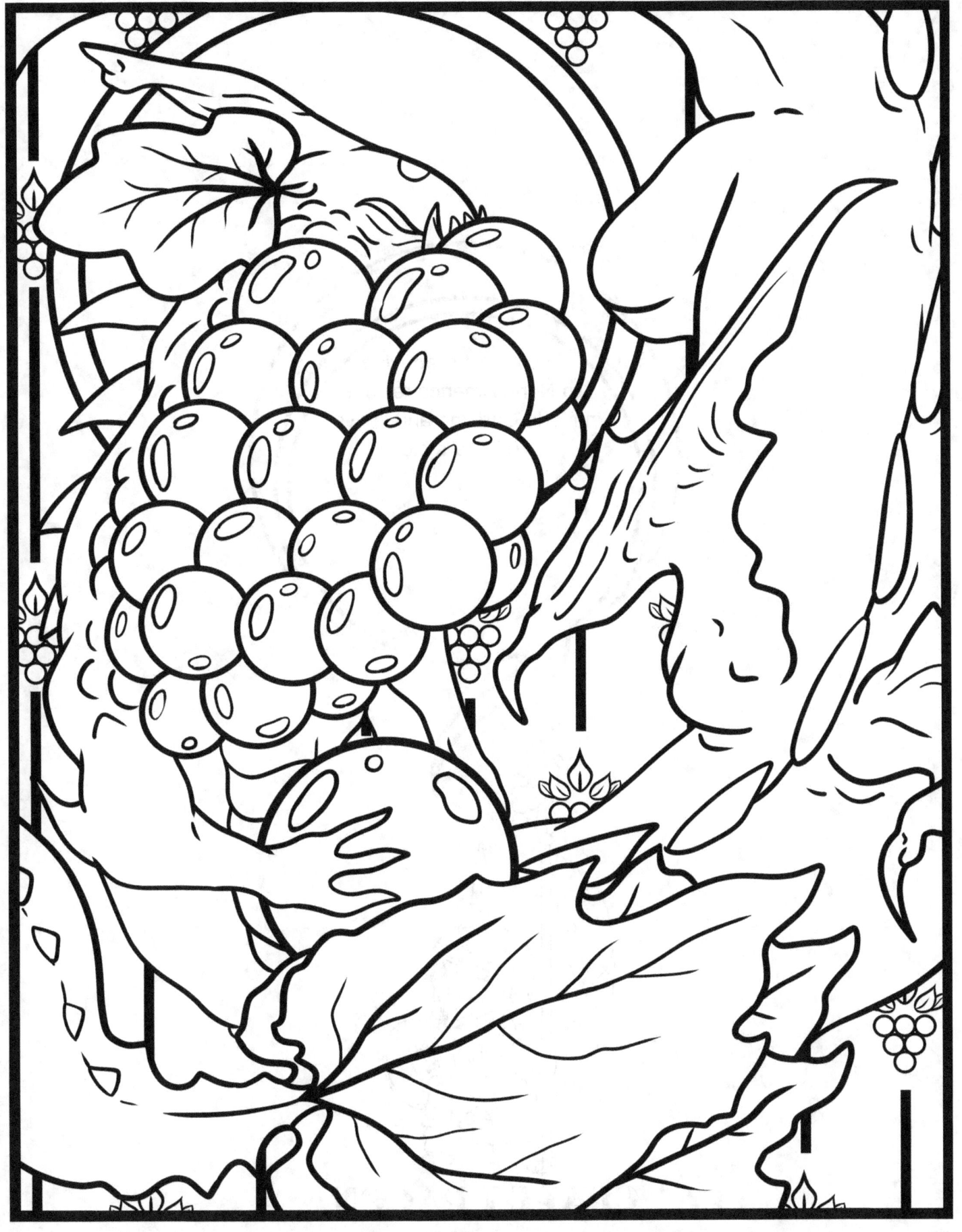

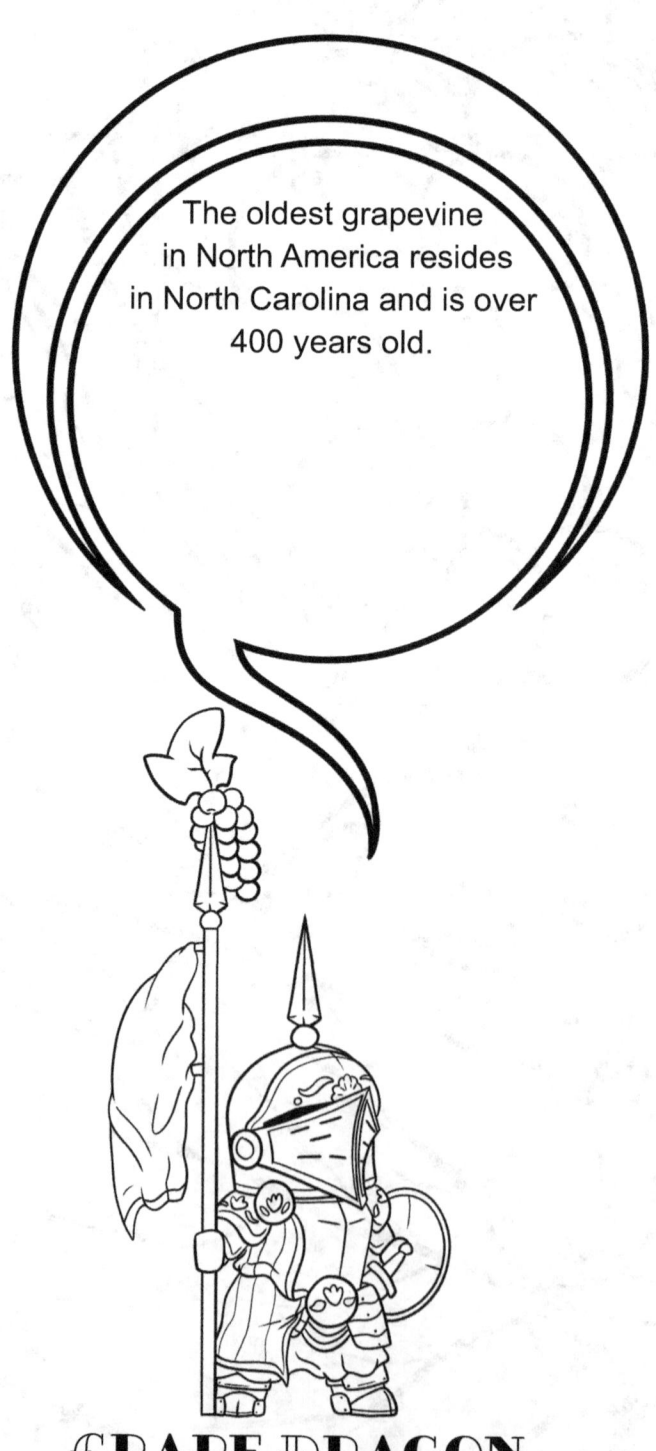

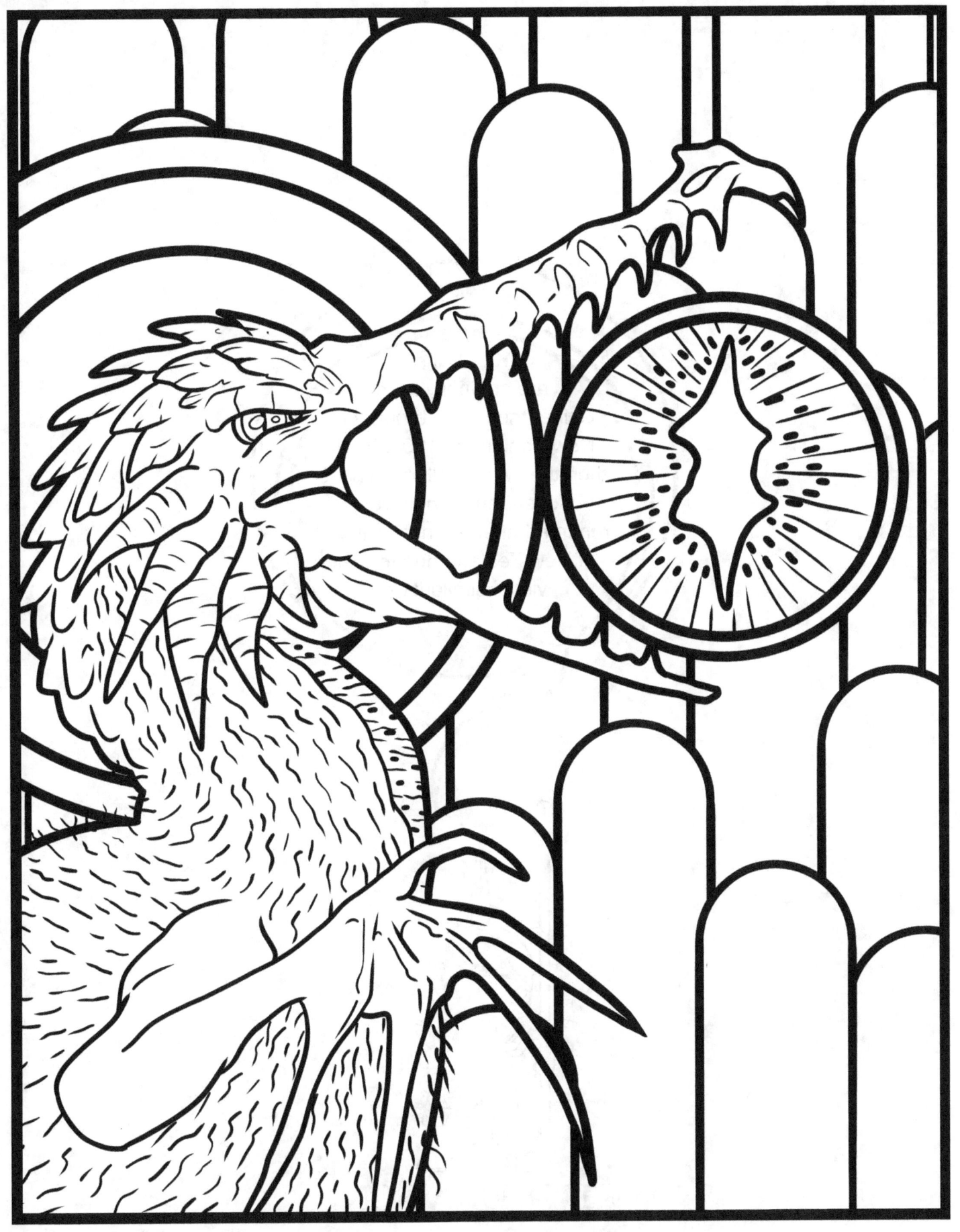

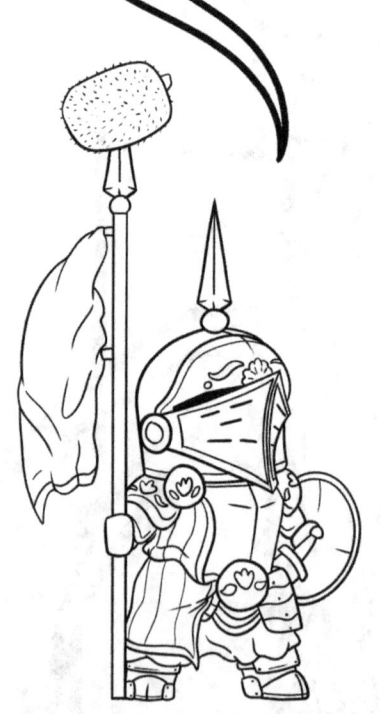

Kiwi fruits are originally from China, they were brought to New Zealand in 1904. Back then they were called Chinese Gooseberry. They were renamed after the national bird of New Zealand due to their visual similarities.

KIWI DRAGON

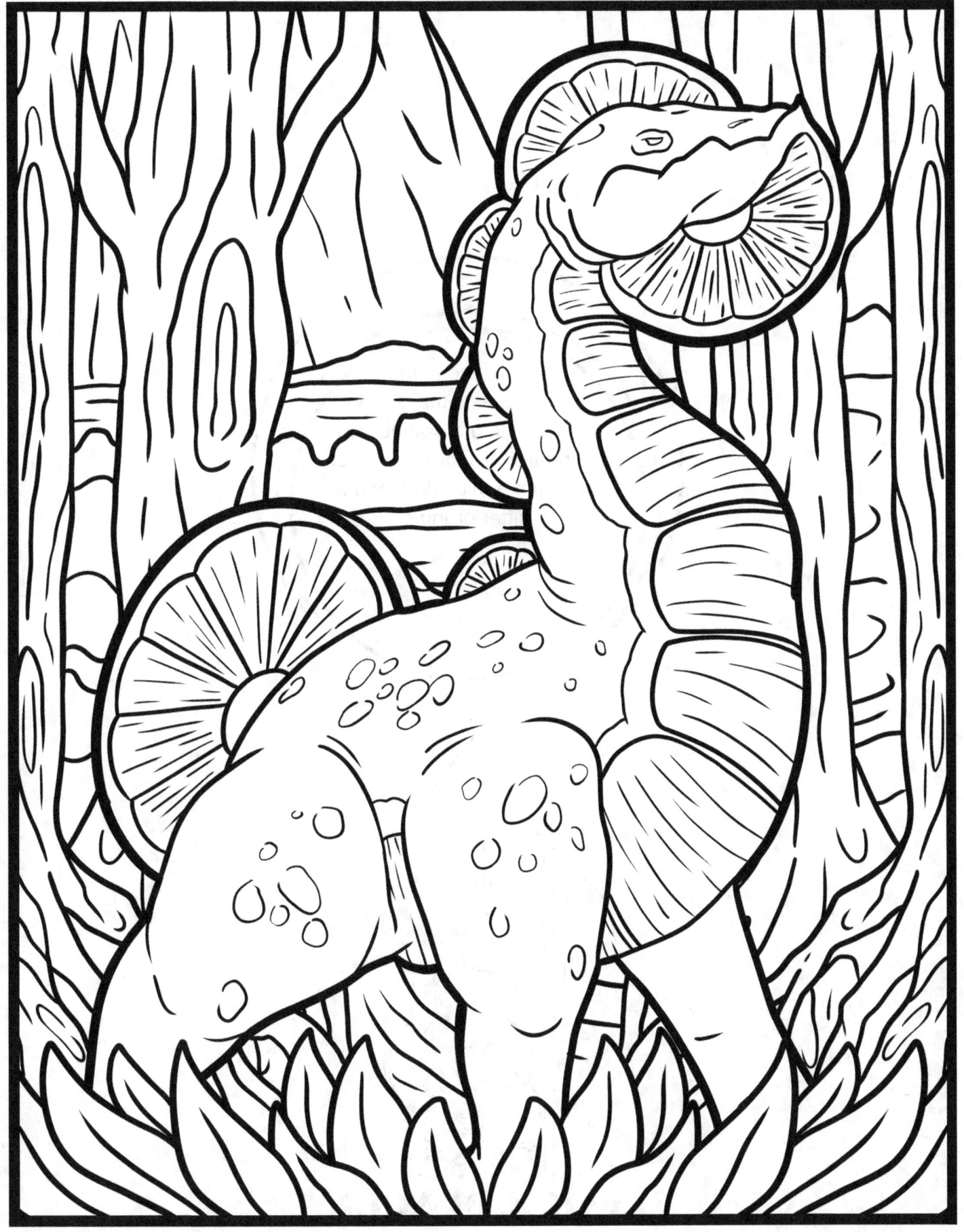

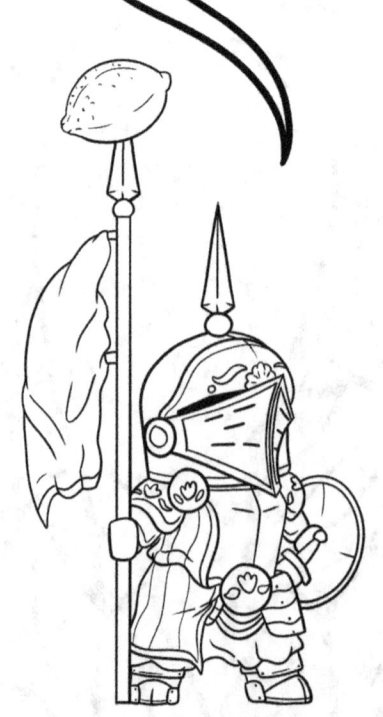

LEMON DRAGON

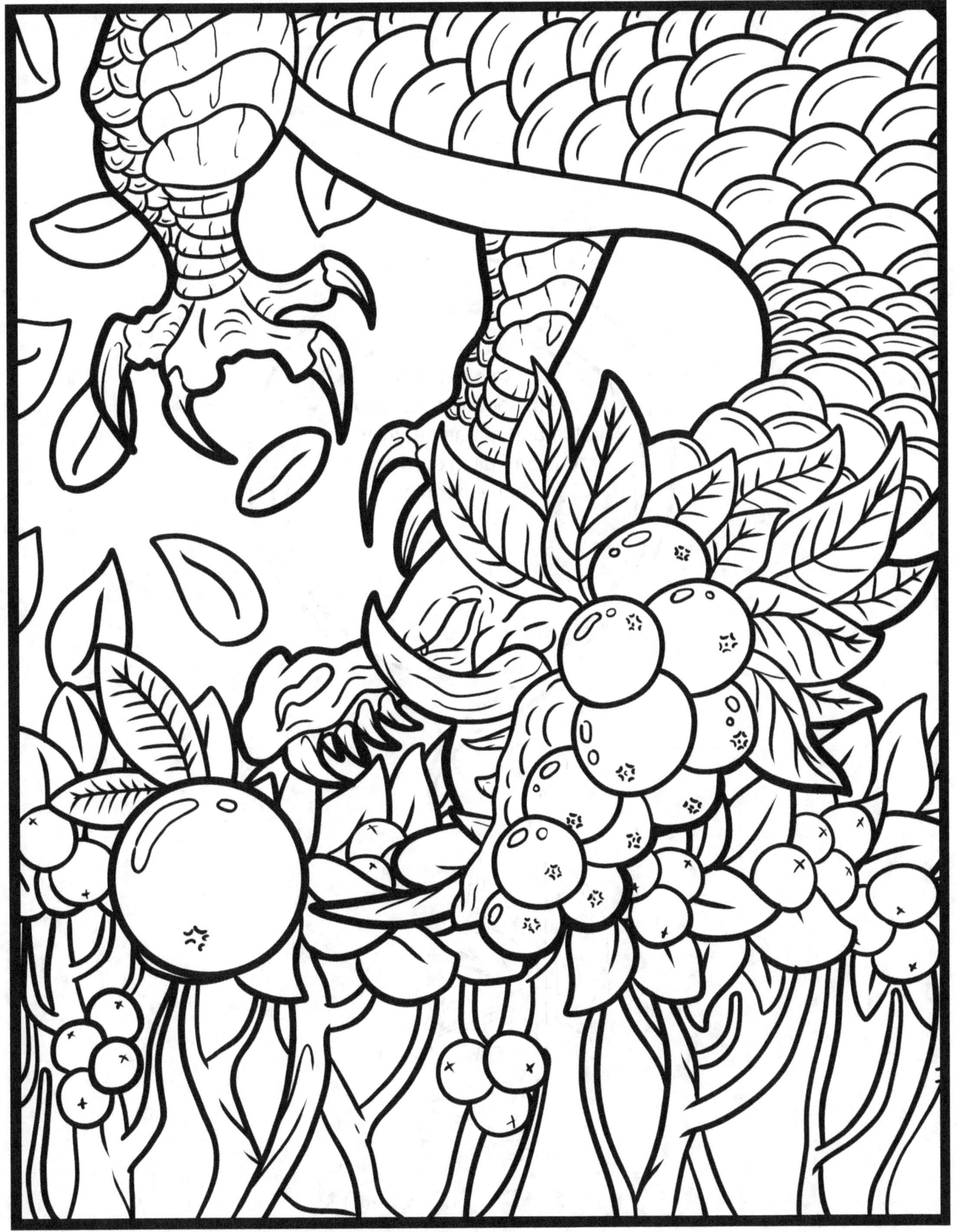

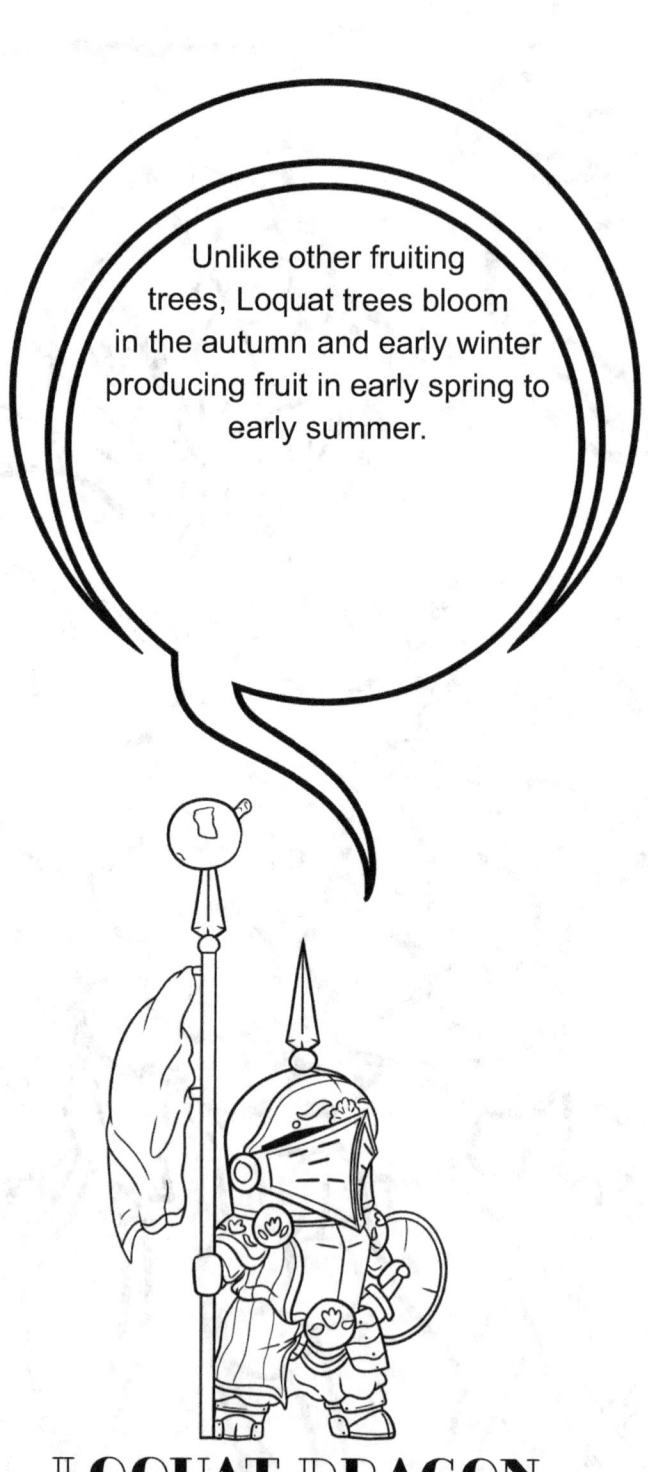

LOQUAT DRAGON

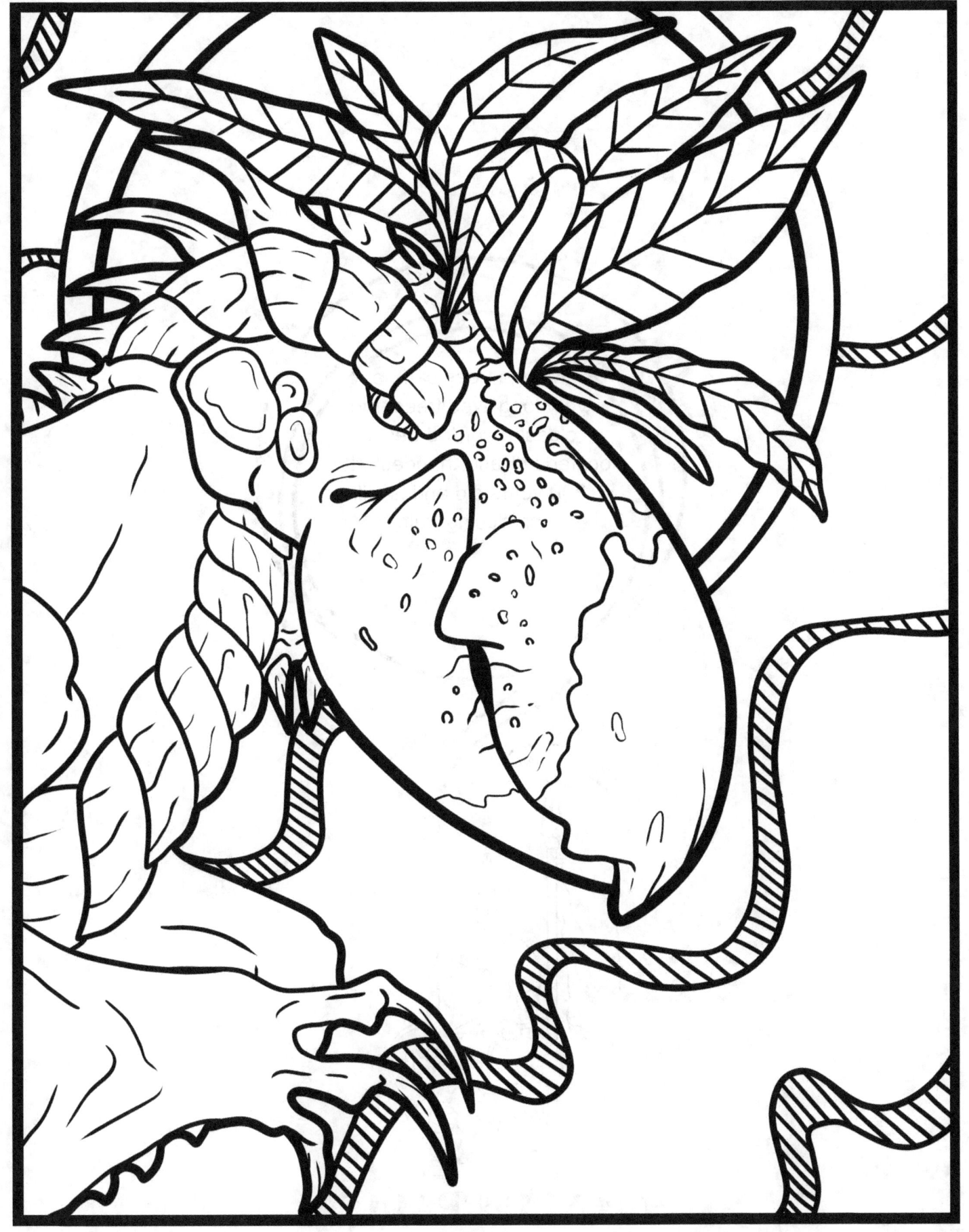

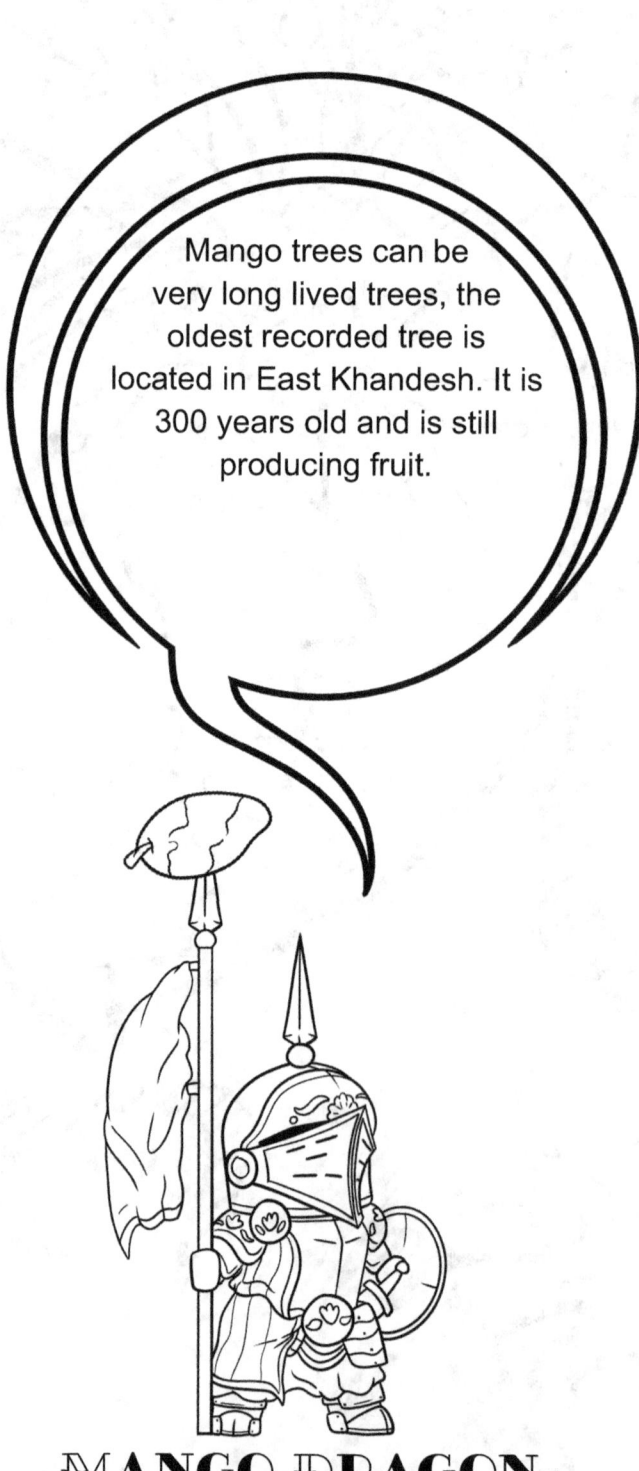

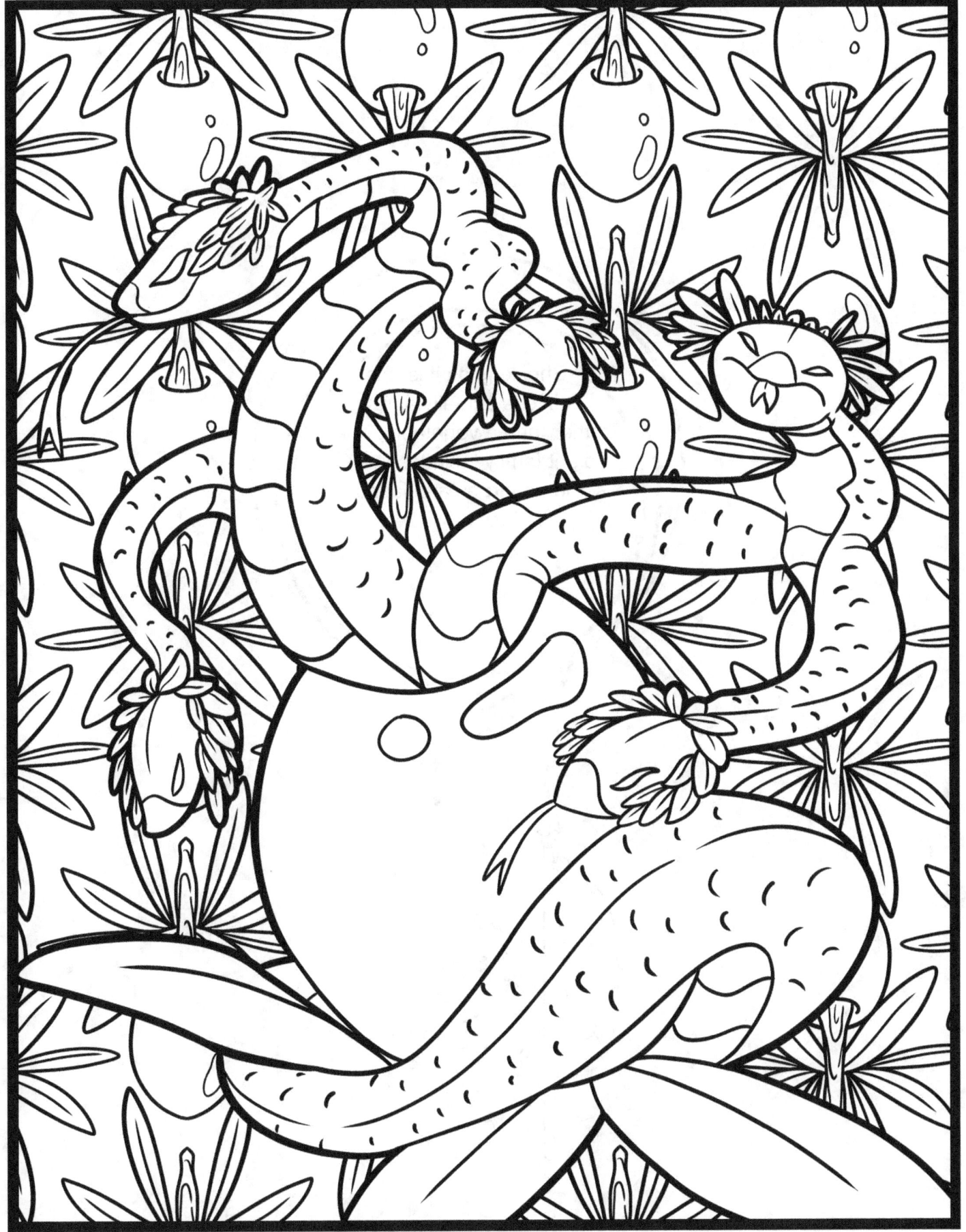

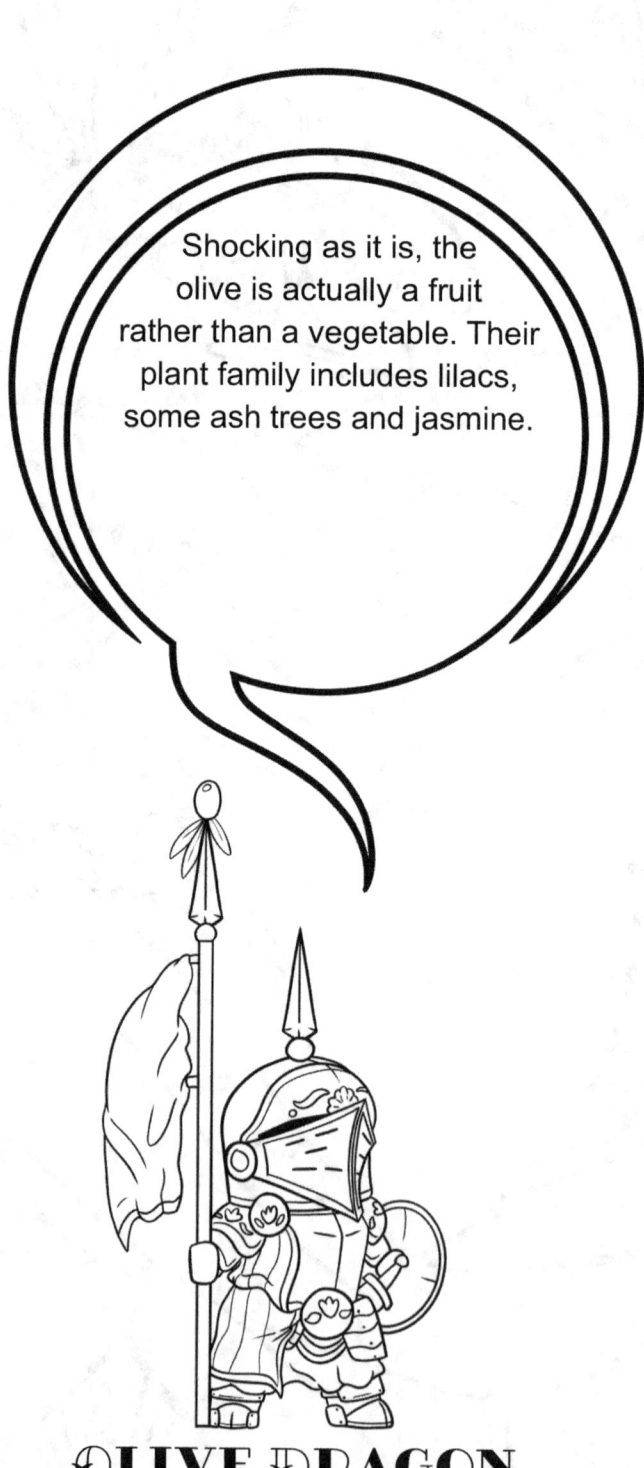

Shocking as it is, the olive is actually a fruit rather than a vegetable. Their plant family includes lilacs, some ash trees and jasmine.

OLIVE DRAGON

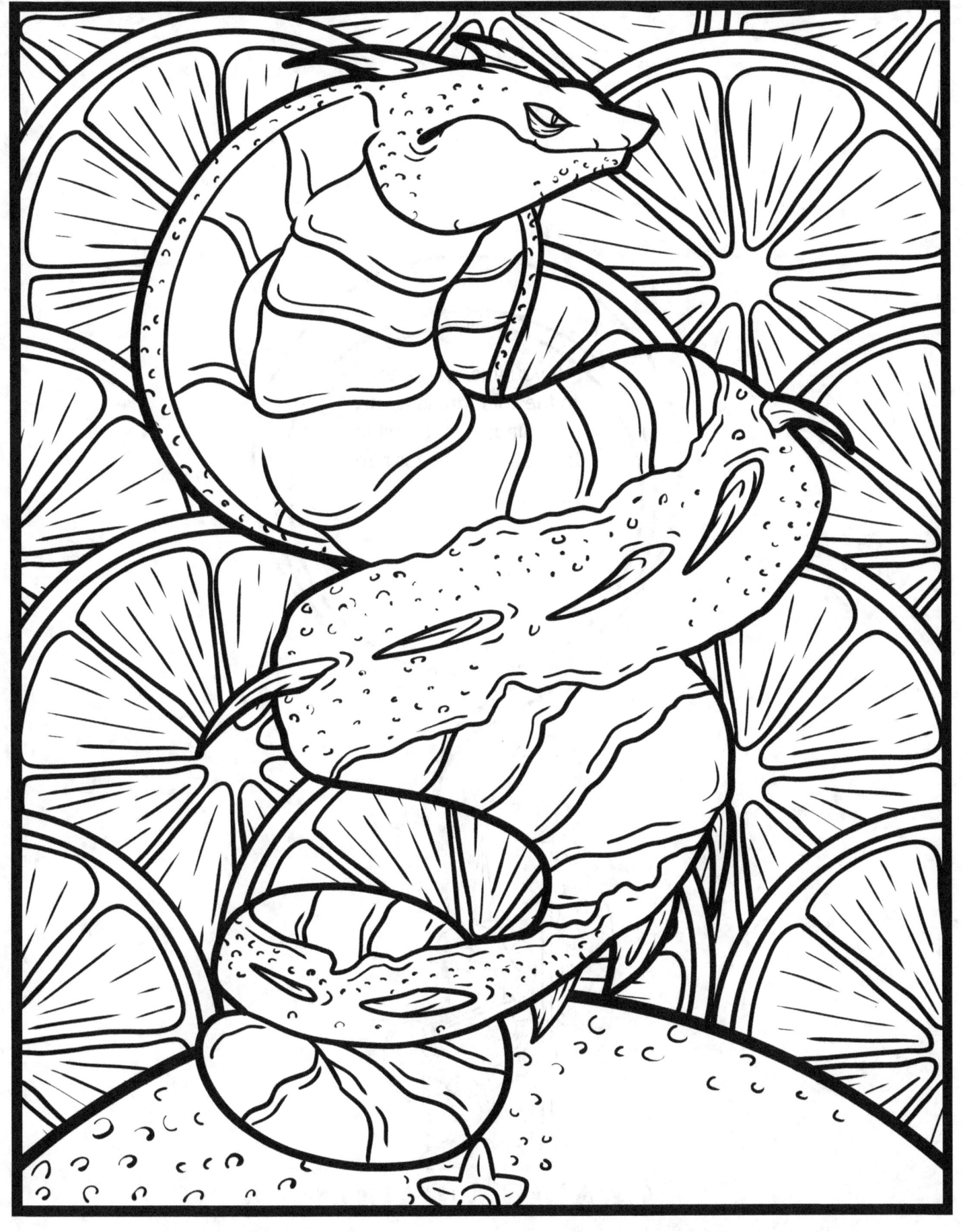

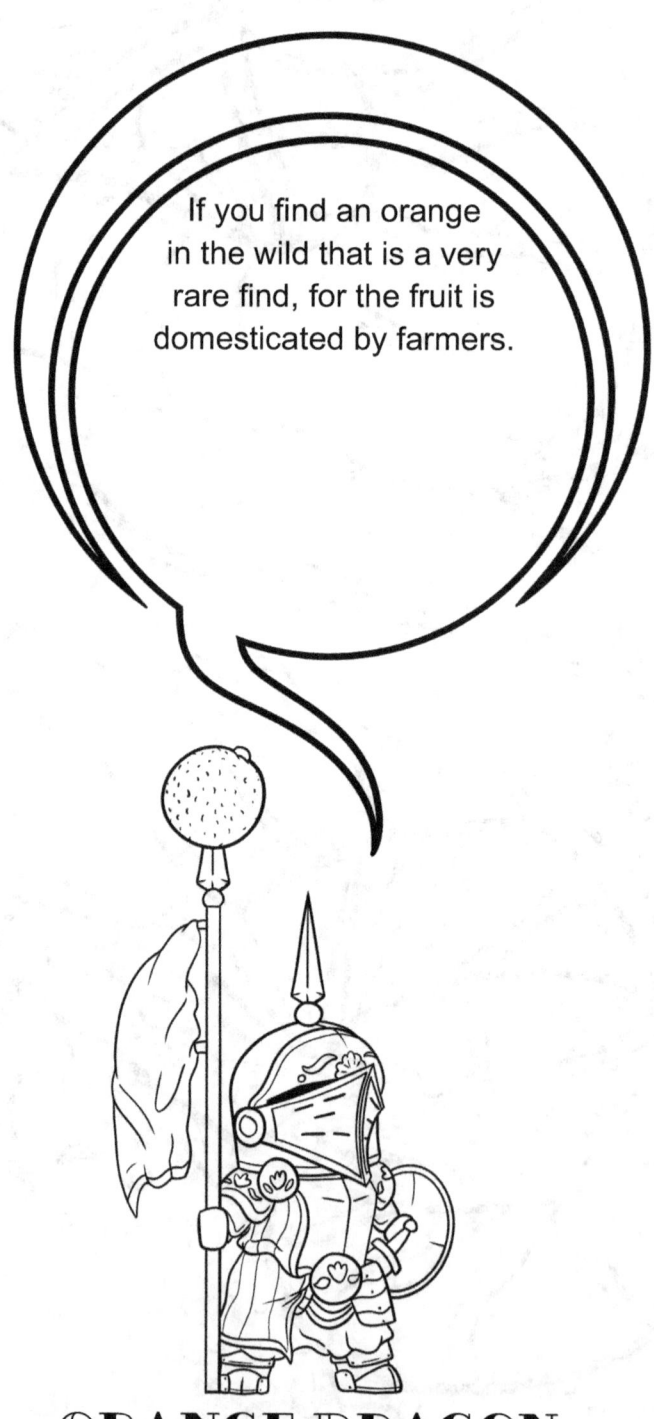

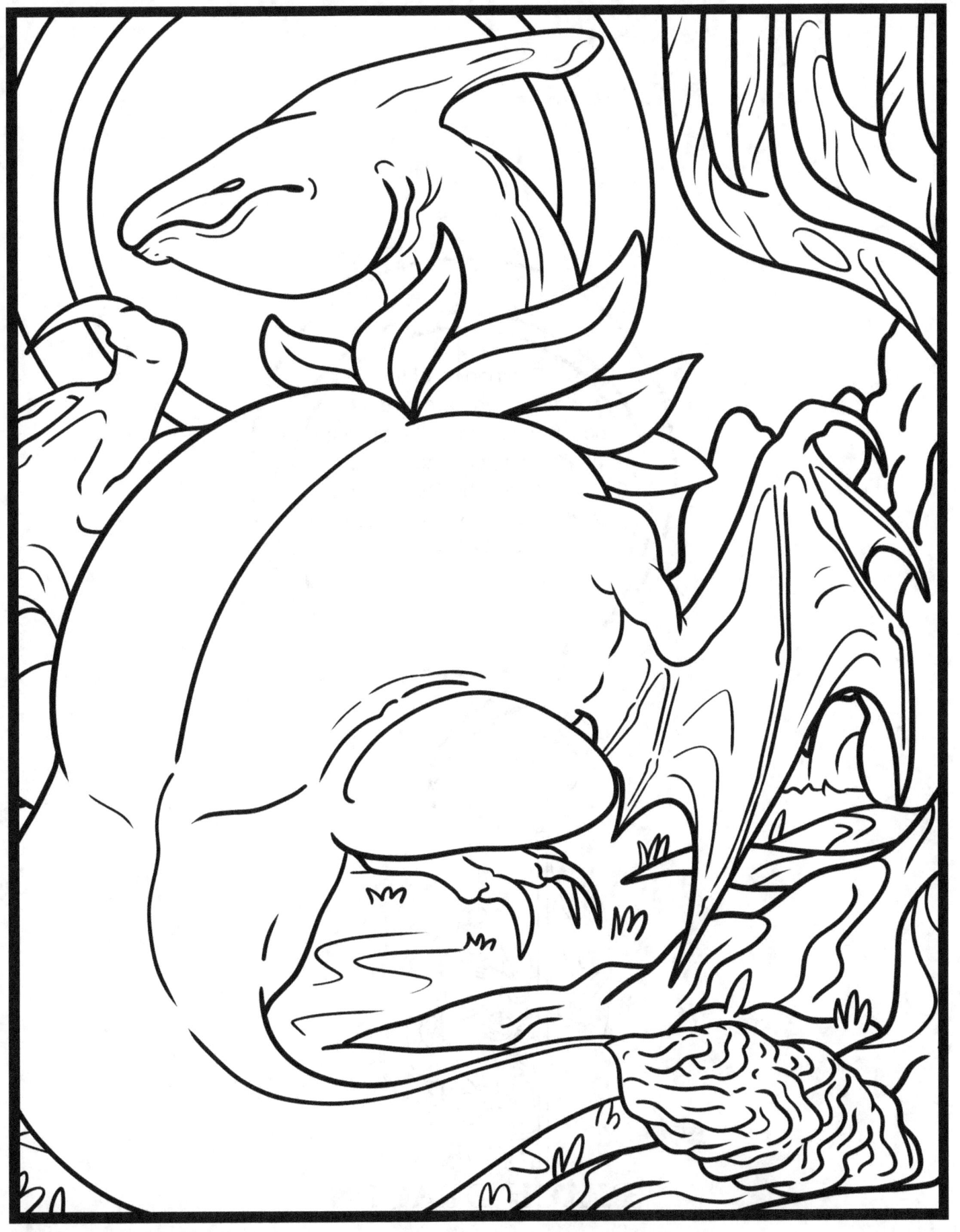

> The origins of the term, "you are a real peach" come from the practice of gifting a peach to a favored friend. Peaches have been used as a compliment since the 1700s.

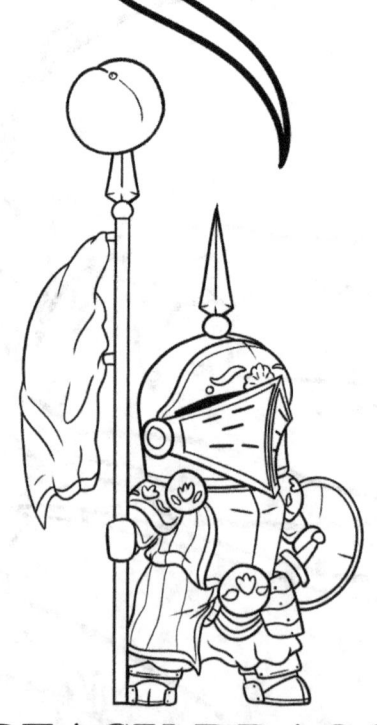

PEACH DRAGON

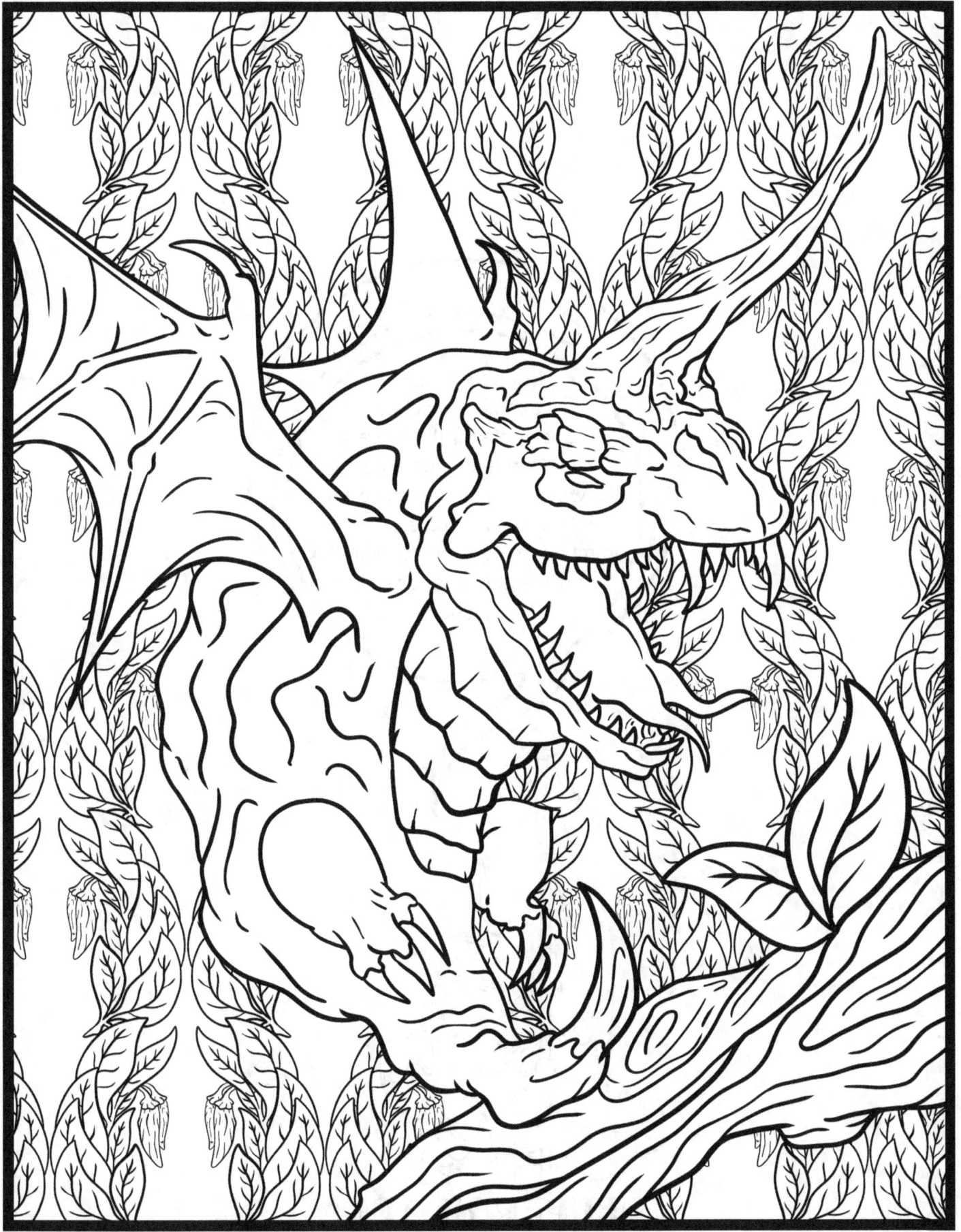

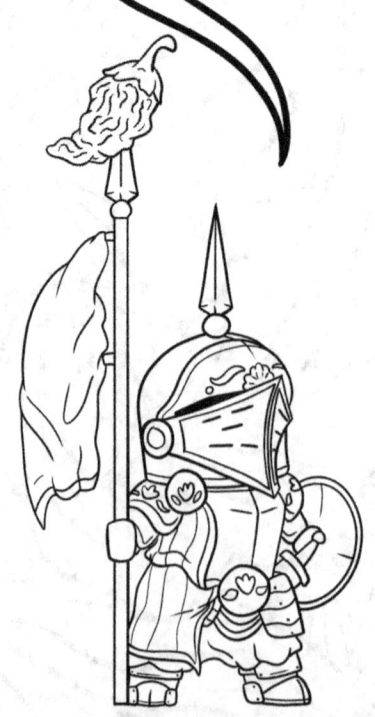

> Peppers contain capsaicin which is responsible for the fire and heat we feel once eaten. However; capsaicin only burns the flesh of mammals, birds are immune and are responsible for spreading the seeds of the plant.

PEPPER DRAGON

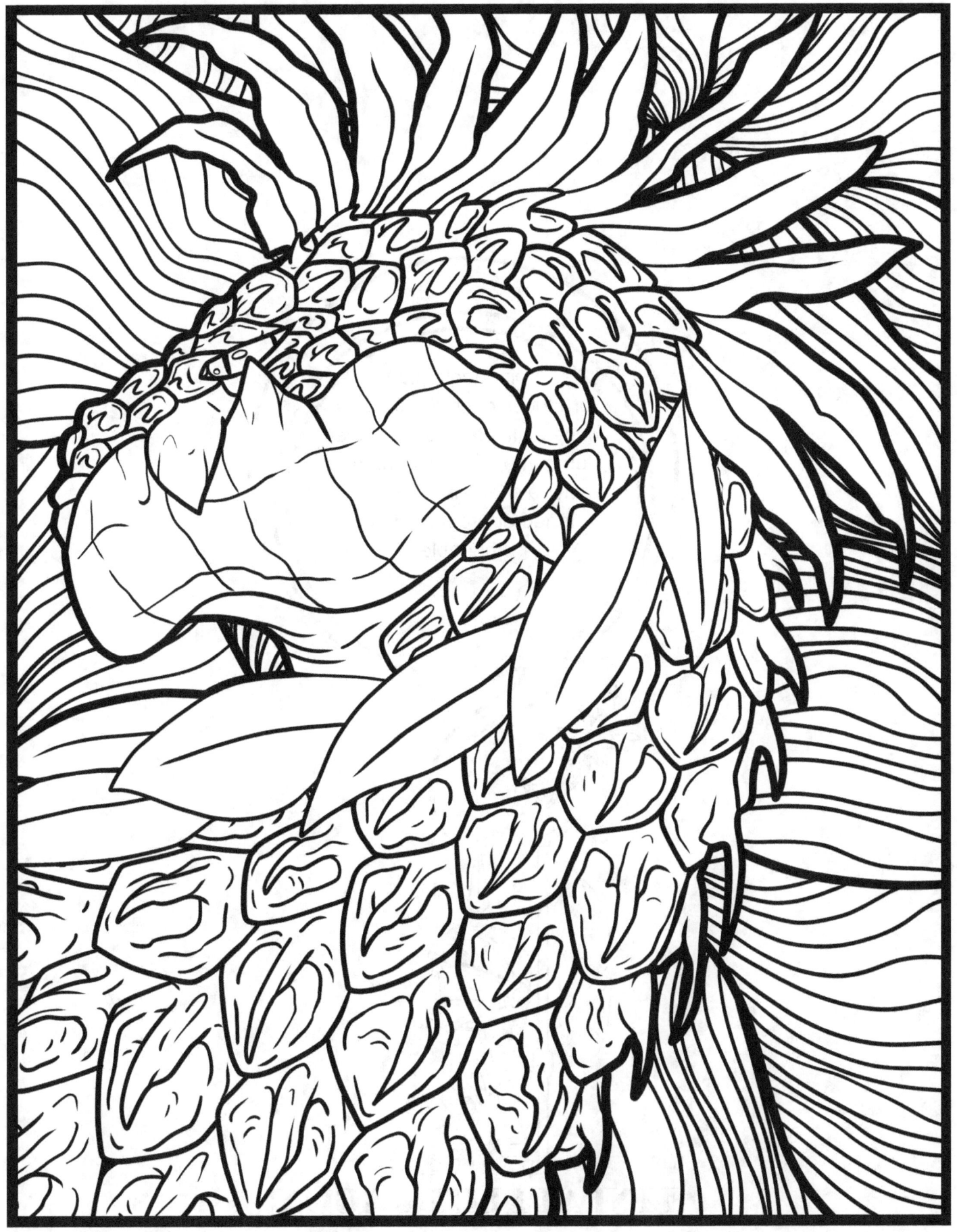

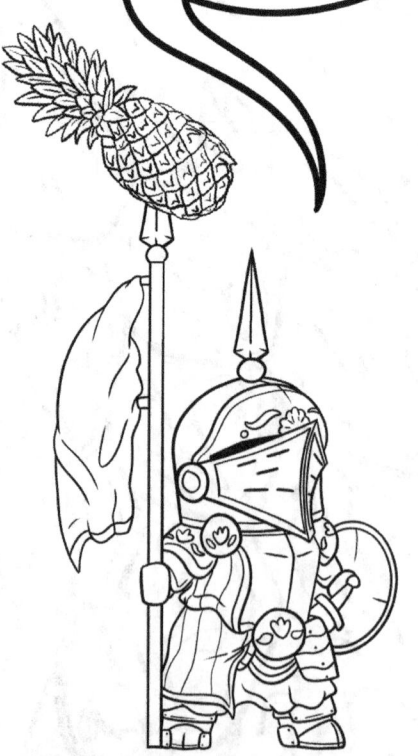

> A pineapple plant produces over 200 flowers once pollinated. Each flower turns into an individual fruit with a scale-like edge, all together producing one pineapple.

PINEAPPLE DRAGON

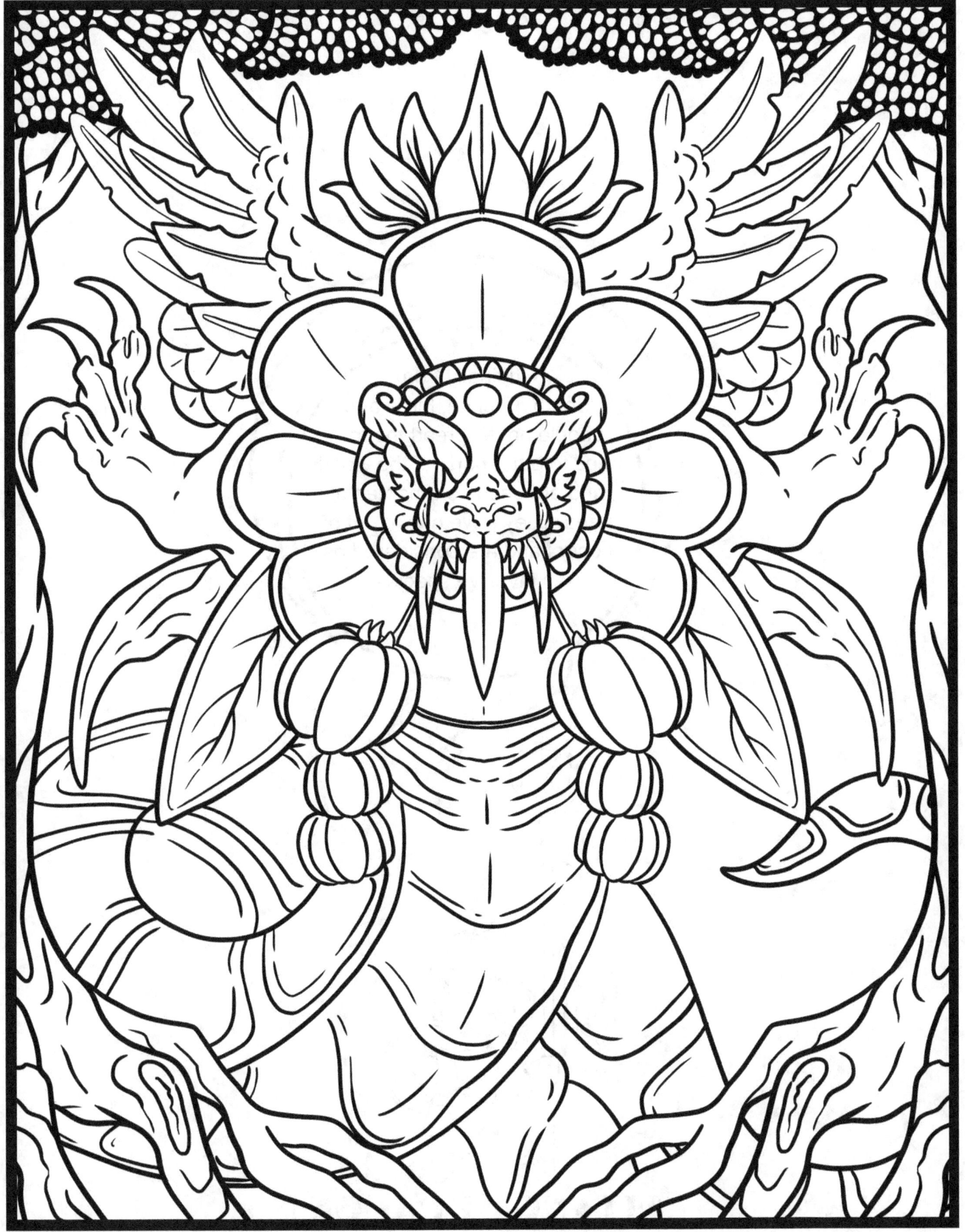

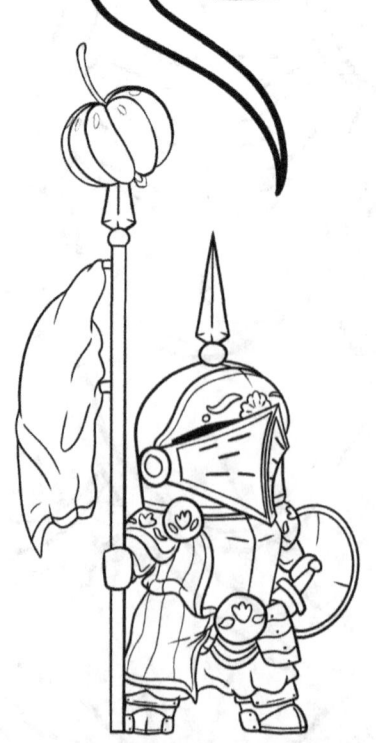

> Originally from South America, birds and people have spread the fruit trees to other parts of the world, and are used as ornamental trees. They have grown out of control and are considered as an invasive species.

PITANGA DRAGON

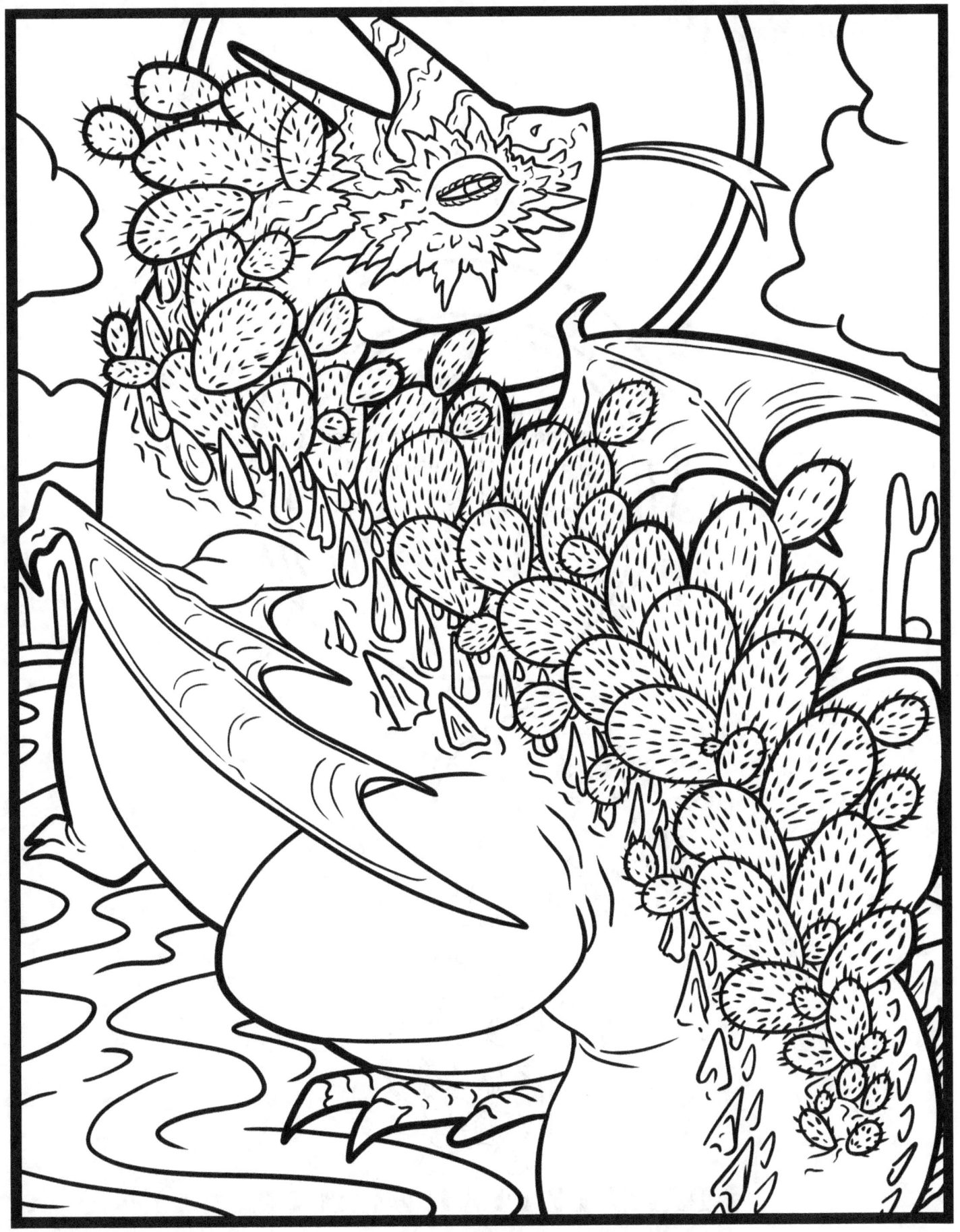

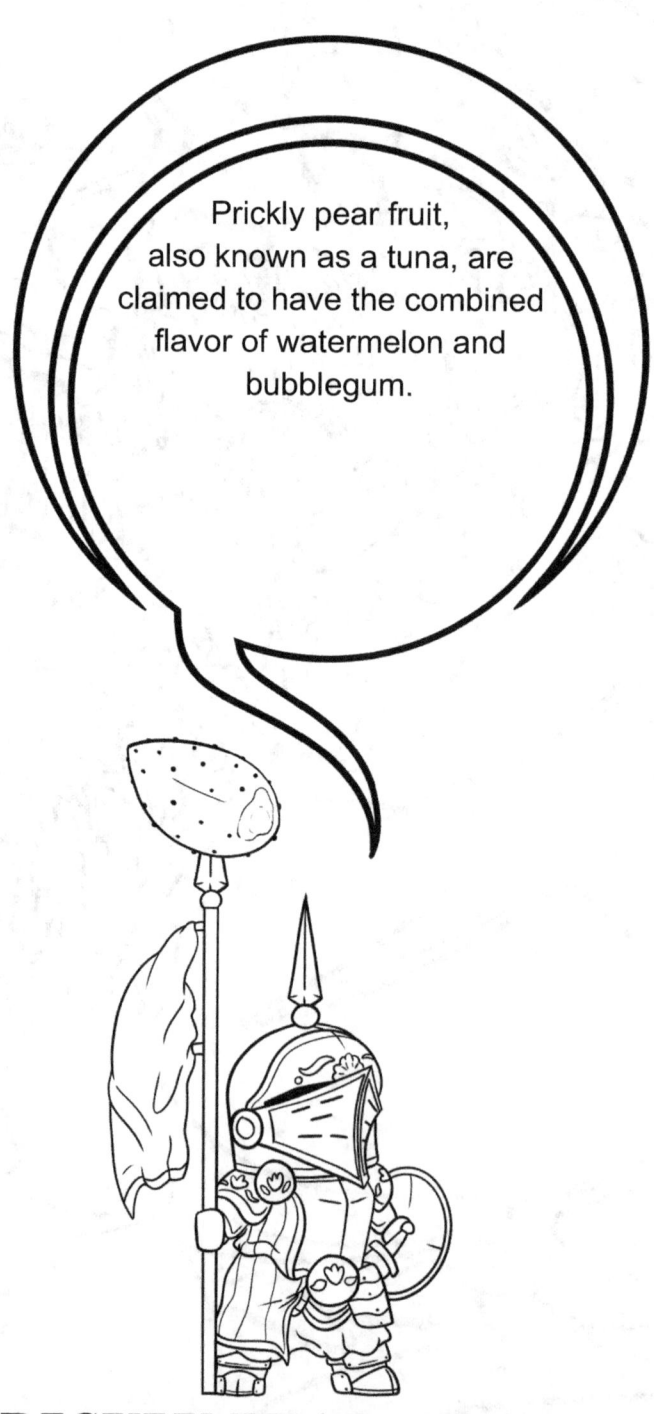

PRICKLY PEAR DRAGON

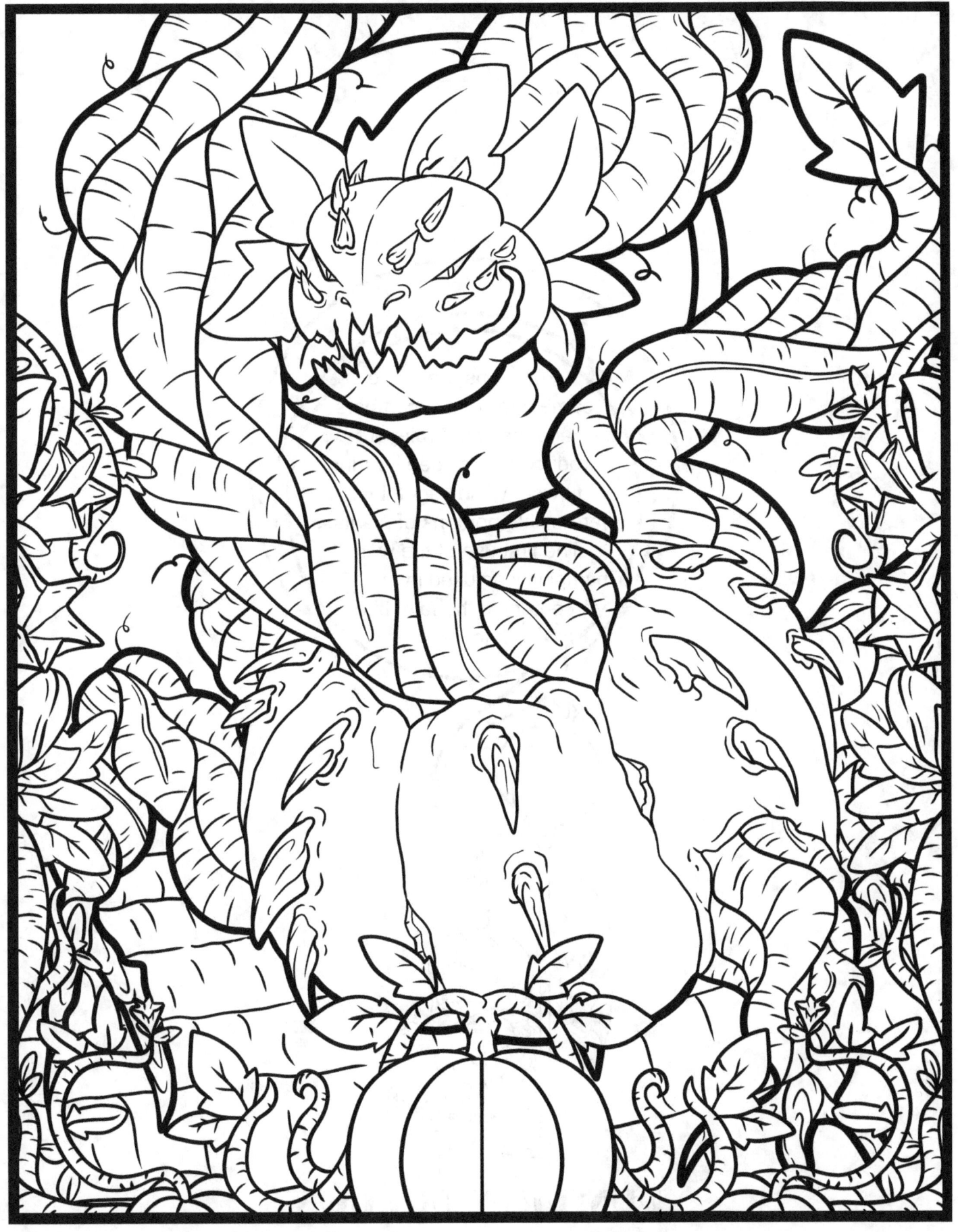

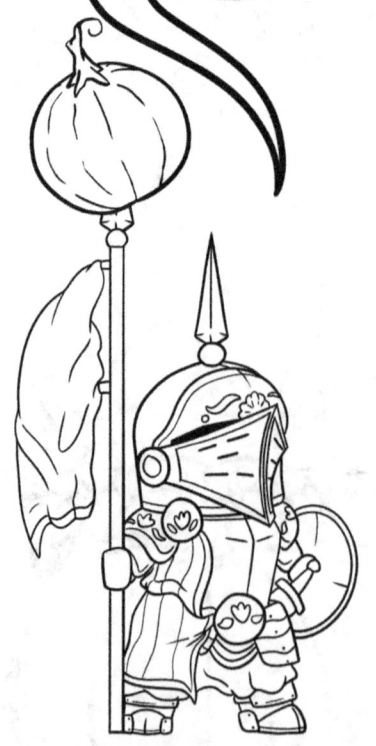

PUMPKIN DRAGON

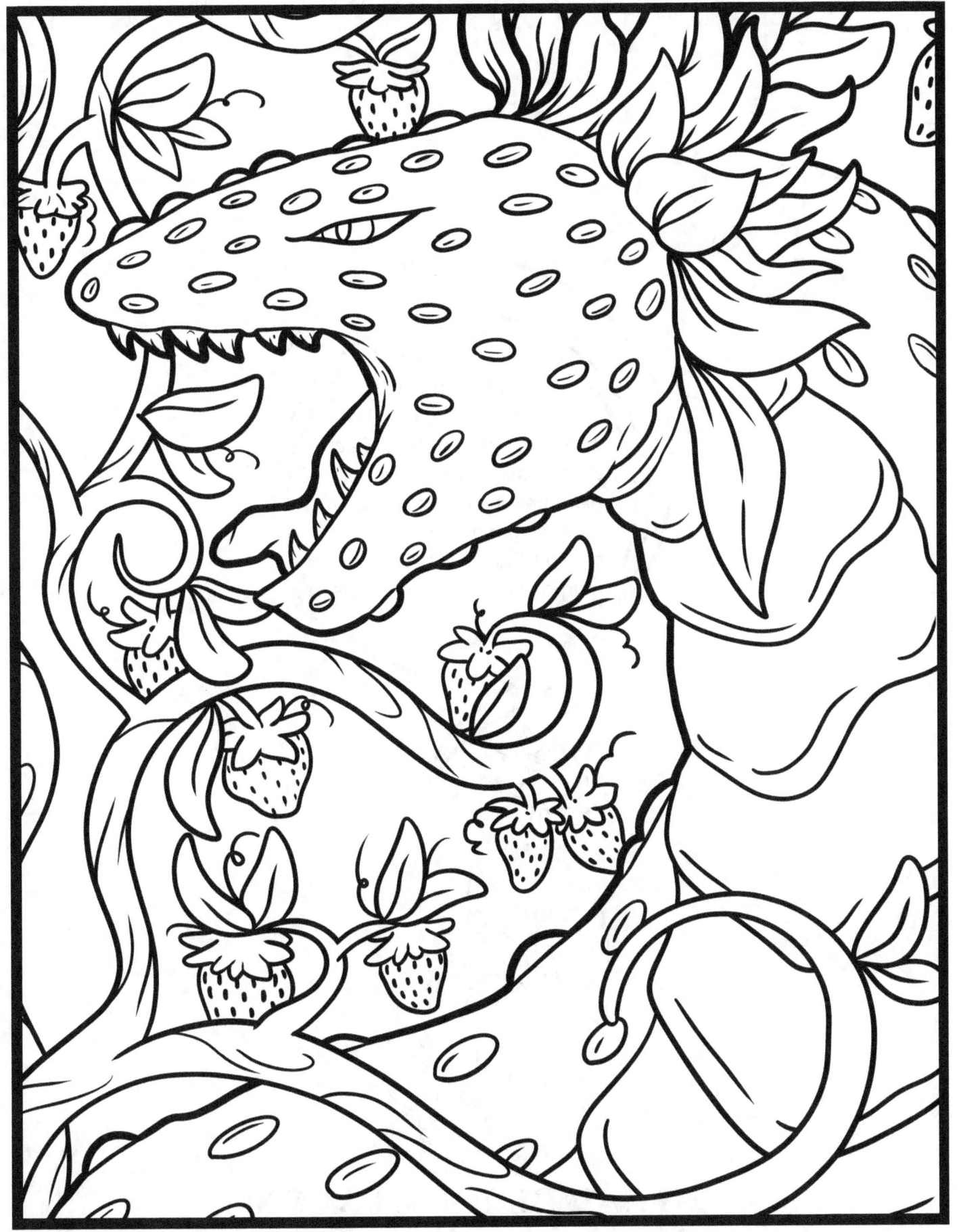

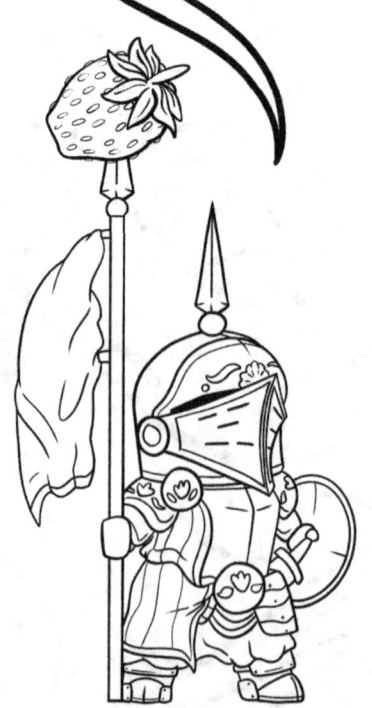

Strawberries are very odd in that they have their seeds on the Outside, unlike berries. Each seed is actually the fruit of the plant and the red flesh we eat is nothing more than swollen, red tissue which has the purpose of holding the fruits.

STRAWBERRY DRAGON

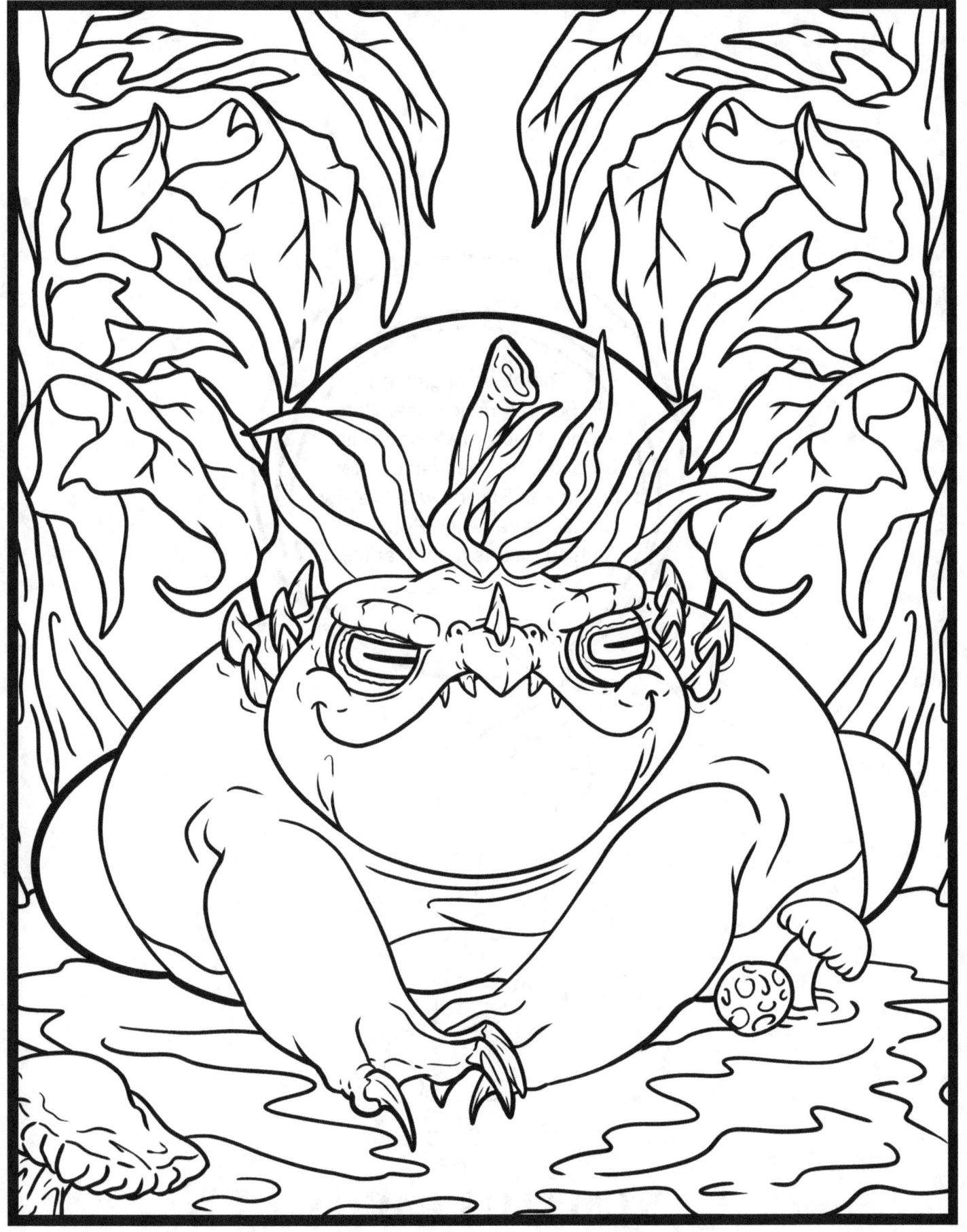

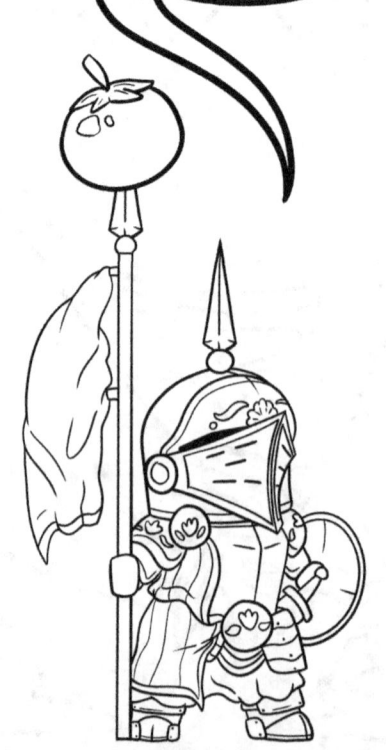

Tomatoes originated in South America near Peru and Southern Mexico. It is believed that the first tomatoes to come to Europe were yellow, for they were called Pomo d'oro which means golden apple.

TOMATO DRAGON

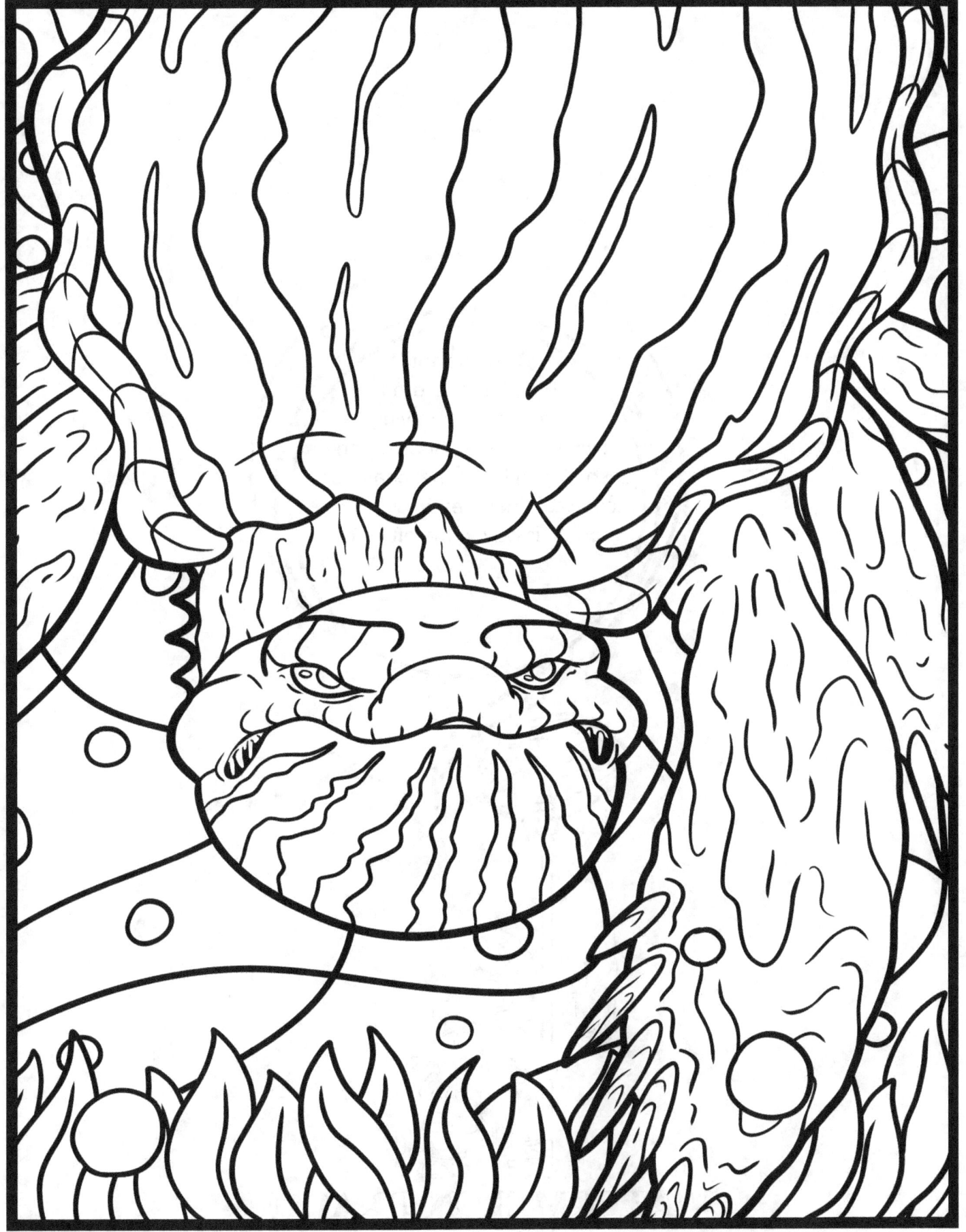

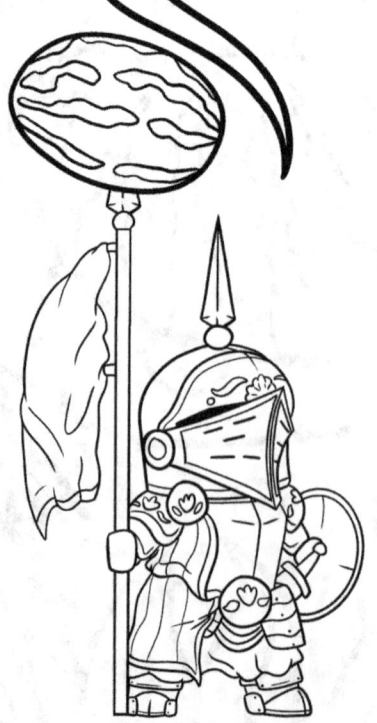

The ancient Egyptians revered watermelon, serving it with salty feta cheese. They also placed it in burial chambers to refresh their dead, who were on their way to the afterlife.

WATERMELON DRAGON

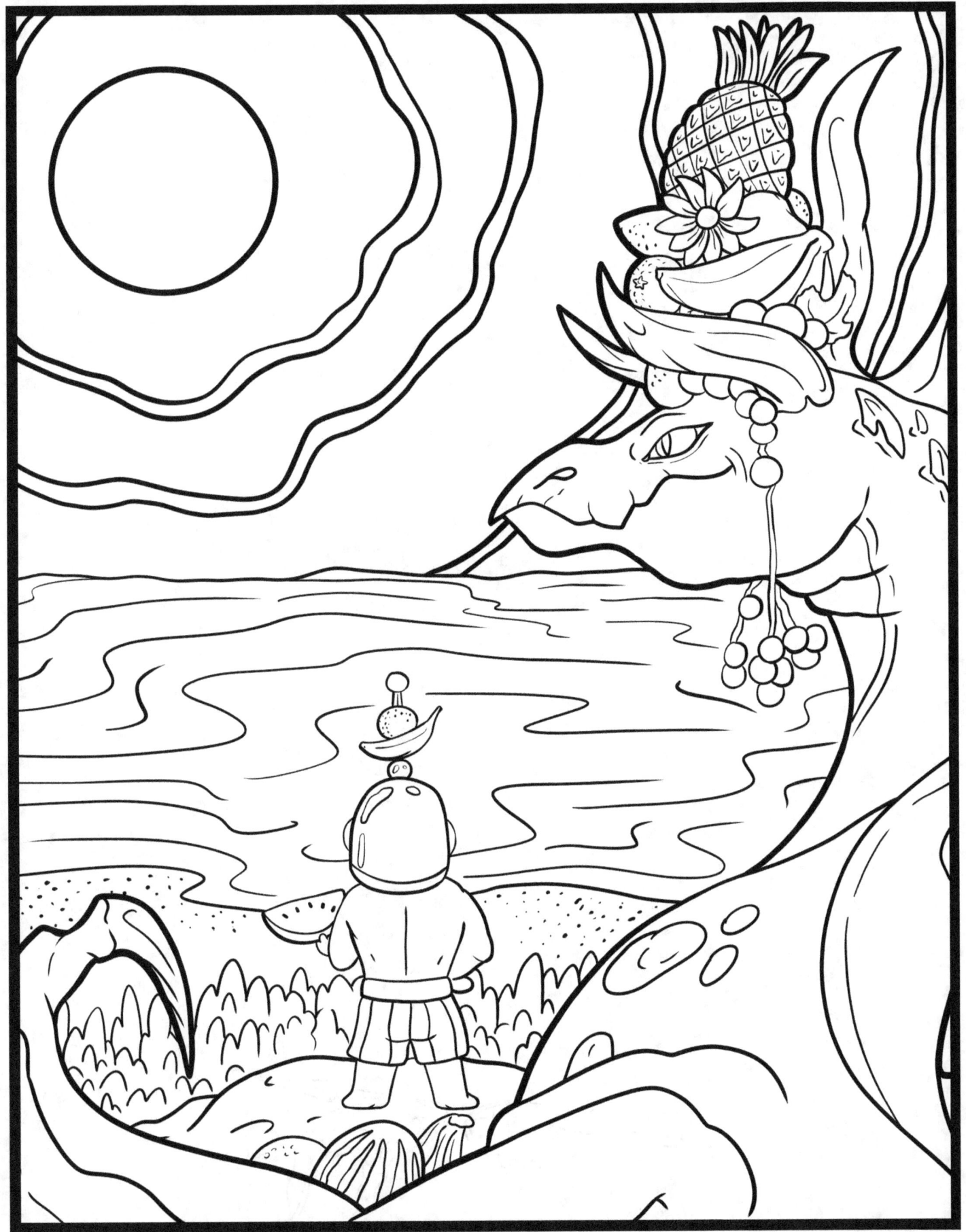

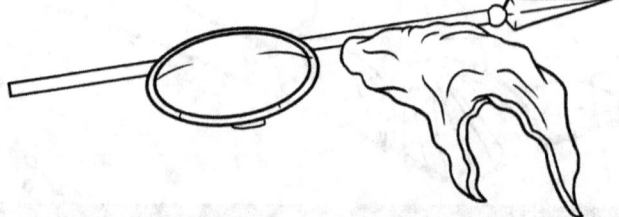

www.ingramcontent.com/pod-product-compliance
Lightning Source LLC
Chambersburg PA
CBHW080525220526
45465CB00006B/2606